Be an Explorer. Not a Tourist.

...and Travel With Integrity.

It feels good to support the people and places in this book.
We are about to introduce you to good people,
good places and good businesses that deserve your time.

ALEXA WEST GUIDES

Cambodia, New Edition 2022

Copyright © 2022 The Solo Girl's Travel Guide

All rights reserved. No part of this publication may be reproduced or copied or transmitted in any form, physical or electronic, or recorded without prior permission from The Solo Girl's Travel Guide ™

Please contact us at hello@thesologirlstravelguide.com

The Solo Girl's Travel Guide updates this book series year-round, as businesses grow, change, and even sometimes, close. A quick double-check before you drive an hour to a restaurant is always a safe practice - as these things are out of our control. And hey, if you see a change we should know about – we'd love it if you let us know so we can update our guide for future travelers.

STOCK OUR BOOK

Want to stock our book in your shop, store, or platform? Send us a message at hello@thesologirlstravelguide.com

Cover photo by @VinceGX

the SOLO GIRL'S  TRAVEL GUIDE

CAMBODIA

ALEXA WEST GUIDES

EVERY GIRL SHOULD TRAVEL SOLO AT LEAST ONCE IN HER LIFE

You don't need a boyfriend, a travel partner or anyone's approval to travel the world. And you don't need a massive bank account or an entire summer off work.

All you need is that wanderlust in your blood and a good guidebook in your hands.

If you've doubted yourself for one moment, remember this:

Millions of girls travel across the globe all by themselves every damn day and you can, too.

You are just as capable, just as smart, and just as brave as the rest of us. You don't need permission – this is your life.

Listen to your gut, follow your heart and remember that the best adventures start with the simple decision to go.

What travelers are saying...

"Alexa West gives you all the knowledge, courage, and confidence you need for taking a solo trip to Cambodia for any solo traveler. She has lived in Cambodia for years and gives you many options suited for all budgets, and experiences. As someone who has all her books… her expertise and guidance makes it possible to take a trip like this feeling confident that it can be done as a solo woman traveler…Alexa West gives so many great options and ideas because she is a local expert.…Thank you Alexa West for yet another amazing travel guide on "Cambodia" The Solo Girl's Travel Guide and inspiring and empowering all of us solo women travelers . I hope you will do an audio book next!"

- Traveler Girl

"I just love reading The Solo Girl's Travel Guide series. They are so easy to read and informative with lots of great insider tips to save you time and direct you to where you are really interested in going. I just want to get on a plane and go explore and be a nomad. Looking forward to the next in Alexa's series…keep them coming! Another country for my bucket list. Thanks Alexa- great job!"

- Dee Wanderlust

"Cambodia is an amazing country but I found it hard to navigate when I was there the first time. Upon wanting to give it another go I went in search of a book that could best suit my needs as a solo traveler and someone who gets a bit daunted by well....lots of things! This book lays out all the information you need to get there, have fun while you're there and explore new and interesting parts of Cambodia. I'm so stoked to go back armed with this book!"

- Jasetyn

Nice to meet you!
I'm Lexi...

I'm not here to get rich or reach 1 million followers on Instagram. I'm here because I want to change the way we travel as women.

I want to help you find yourself.

I want to fling you to the other side of the world, out of your comfort zone (but still safe, I got you), and help you get so totally lost that you find yourself.

And I do that by connecting you to the most beautiful places, the kindest people, the most challenging opportunities, and the most rewarding experiences.

Do you know what kind of woman this will create?

A happy woman who shines so bright that everyone she comes in contact with is illuminated too.

I'm here to turn your light up, girl.

I'm here to help you connect to the experiences that will change you. … and get the best Instagram photos, too, of course.

To glow up on your travels, remember Travel Karma is real and beautiful.

A LITTLE ABOUT ME

Back in 2010, I was a broke-ass Seattle girl who had just graduated from college and had about $200 to my name. I was faced with two choices: get a job, a husband, and have 3 babies plus a mortgage…or sell everything I owned, travel the world and disappoint my parents.

Obviously, I made the right choice.

For the past 10 years, I've been traveling the world solo. I've played every travel role from being the young volunteer and broke backpacker to flying to exotic islands to review new luxury hotels and give breath to struggling tourism industries.

Now I spend my days as an explorer on a mission to change the way that women travel the world. I want to show you places you've never seen and unlock hidden doors you never knew existed in places you may have been before. I want to create a path for you where you feel safe while diving deeper into cultures and countries beyond your own – whether for a week, a year, or a lifetime. And that's what I'm doing.

xoxo, Alexa West

Flights, airports, walking around town…
Travel is a little bit more magical when good music is involved.
Find my Cambodia playlist here.

ALEXA'S #1 TIP FOR MAKING FRIENDS AS A SOLO TRAVELER

Put your damn phone down.

You didn't come all the way here just to scroll on Instagram, now did you?

People are less likely to approach you when you look so busy on your phone. You have no shot of making eye contact with a stranger if you're staring at reading internet gossip. You miss every opportunity that you do not see.

The next time you're sitting at a bar or on the beach and you have nothing to entertain you, resist the urge to pick up your phone. Resist the addiction. Instead, journal while taking time to look around. Listen to music with one headphone in. Or just sit and watch people walking by.

Hell, next time you need directions, put the phone down. Ask a human. Give yourself every chance to make human contact and watch your world spin into beautiful circumstances you never could have planned.

WANT MORE TRAVEL TIPS?

Join Alexa's travel tip email series. This will change how you travel forever.

Go to TheSoloGirlsTravelGuide.com and sign-up for her newsletter.

Don't forget your map!

To keep the price of this book affordable for you,
there are no fancy detailed maps inside.

I've got something even better.

SCAN THE CODE below to get your interactive
CAMBODIA MAP that you can travel with on the **AREA.**

TABLE OF CONTENTS

Introduction to Cambodia 15
The Mini Cambodia
Bucket List 19
Your Cambodia Bucket List 21

Cambodia Survival Guide 22
    Quick Things to Consider 23
    Weather in Cambodia................24
    Tourist Visa................................26
    What to Pack 30
    How to Budget 34
    Internet & Data.........................40
    Khmer Language Guide...........42
    Transporation 46
    Safe Girl Tips & Advice 52

Chapter 1: Phnom Penh............60
    Introduction to Phnom Penh 61
    Areas to Explore...........................62
    Where to Stay............................... 64
    Where to Eat................................67
    Sights & History 70
    Fun Things to Do.........................74
    Shopping (and more eating)
    in Phnom Penh 76
    Spas & Salons 78
    Nightlife 79
    How to Get Around 80

Crime & Safety............................81
How to Get to Phnom Penh 82
From the Phnom Penh
Airport into Town 86

Chapter 2: Siem Reap 88
    Introduction to Siem Reap 89
    Where to Stay..............................91
    Where to Eat...............................94
    Sights & History 96
    Fun Things to Do.......................102
    Shopping in Siem Reap 104
    Spas & Salon..............................105
    Nightlife 106
    How to Get Around 108
    How to Get to Siem Reap 110
    From the Airport to Siem Reap..114

Chapter 3: Battambang..........116
    Introduction to Battambang 117
    Where to Stay.............................118
    Where to Eat..............................120
    Sights & History 123
    Fun Things to Do.......................126
    Shopping 128
    How to Get to Battambang 129

Chapter 4: Kampot 131
    Introduction to Kampot 132
    Where to Stay 134
    Where to Eat 137
    Things to Do 139
    Shopping 143
    How to Get Around Kampot 144
    How to Get to Kampot 145
    Crime & Safety 146

Chapter 5: Sihanoukville 147
    Introduction to Sihanoukville 148
    Where to Stay 150
    Where to Eat 151
    Shopping 152
    Things to Do 153
    Crime & Safety 155
    How to Get
    Around Sihanoukville 156
    How to Get to Sihanoukville 157

Part2: The Islands 161
Chapter 6: Koh Rong 162
    Introduction to Koh Rong 163
    Where to Stay 167
    Things to Do 169
    Nightlife 171
    How to Get Around Koh Rong. 172
    Crime & Safety 172
    How to Get to Koh Rong 173

Chapter 7: Koh Rong Samloem 175
    Introduction to
    Koh Rong Samloem 176
    Where to Stay 178
    Where to Eat 180
    Things to Do 182
    Nightlife 184
    How to Get to
    Koh Rong Samloem 185

Chapter 8: Koh Ta Kiev 186
    Introduction to Koh Ta Tiev 187
    Where to Stay 188
    Where to Eat 189
    Things to Do 189
    How to Get
    to Koh Ta Kiev 191

Volunteering in Cambodia 192
Itineraries for Cambodia 195
How to Get to Other Countries 198
Cambodian
Festivals & Holidays 201
Mini Directory 205
The 11 Travel Commandments of
the Solo Girl's Travel Guide 211

SEE A GIRL TRAVELING WITH THIS GEAR? SAY HI.

SHE'S YOUR SISTER IN THE

Solo Girl's Travel Club

CARRY THIS GEAR
AS AN INVITATION TO FRIENDSHIP

COLLECT YOUR GEAR HERE:

OR AT THESOLOGIRLSTRAVELGUIDE.COM

INTRODUCTION TO
Cambodia

WELCOME TO CAMBODIA

Cambodia is a land of contrasts.

You've got mystical ancient temples in the north, one of the fastest growing cities in the world nestled in the center and a breathtaking collection of virgin beaches in the south. All of which are packed into one tiny country the size of Washington State.

Most tourists come to Cambodia with the sole intention of visiting Angkor Wat - an mystifying temple complex spanning over 400 square kilometers with Tomb Raider style architecture in the middle of the jungle. But this stunning site is only the tip of the iceberg when it comes to experiencing the beauty of Cambodia.

@ALLPHOTOLONDON

Get ready for a well-rounded vacation in this underrated South East Asian country.

Witness the harrowing recent history of the country at Phnom Penh's Killing Fields and S21 prison. A visit not for the faint of heart, but an important piece of this country's puzzle.

Sip sunset cocktails by the river in Kampot, or rent a scooter and drive up the mountain to abandoned French mansions on Bokor Mountain.

Party till dawn with fellow solo travelers and experienced expats on the beaches of Sihanoukville where you can have a complete night out for under $10.

If a digital detox is what you're looking for - check out the island of Koh Ta Kiev, there's no electricity so you can kick back and relax offline for a few days.

And while everyone on Earth knows about Thailand's islands, filling them to the brim with tourists – Cambodia's islands remain relatively unspoiled with white sand and turquoise waters. The tourism clock is ticking...

now is your chance to visit Koh Rong and Koh Rong Samleom before mass tourism takes over in just a few years time.

Whether you've got a few days, a week or even a month – Cambodia is going to make its way into your heart one way or another.

DID YOU KNOW?

There are 61 islands off the coast of Cambodia.

CAMBODIA101

Language: Khmer - but many people speak English

Population: 16.7 Million People

Total Area: 69,898 square miles (almost the same size as Washington State)

Currency: US Dollars and Cambodian Riel

Time Zone: (GMT+7)

Religion: Buddhist

Where: Cambodia sits in the center of Southeast Asia with Cambodia to the west, Loas to the north and Vietnam to the east.

♥ Hey! Do you know how many girls live their whole lives and never even leave their own country?

Look at you go! You're special. Don't forget that.

INTRODUCTION TO CAMBODIA

The Mini Cambodia Bucket List

TOP 10 CAMBODIA EXPERIENCES

01 Angkor Wat, Siem Reap

📷 VICKY.TAO.33

02 The Killing Fields & S21 Tuol Sleng Genocide Museum
03 Elephant Valley Project, Mondulkiri / Sen Monorom
04 The Beaches of Koh Rong Samloem
05 Wander the Night Markets of Siem Reap
06 Stay in a Riverside Bungalow in Kampot
07 Motorbike up Bokor Mountain, Kampot
08 Phare Circus, Siem Reap
09 Swim with Plankton at Night, Koh Rong Samloem
10 Taco Tuesday, Karma Traders Kampot

TOP 10 PLACES TO STAY IN CAMBODIA

 01 Karma Traders, Kampot

02 Meraki, Kampot

 03 Kactus, Koh Ta Kiev

04 Plantation Urban Resort & Spa, Phnom Penh

 05 BeachWalk, Koh Rong

06 SunBoo Beach Bungalows, Koh Rong Samloem

 07 Golden Temple Hotel, Siem Reap

08 Onederz Hostel, Siem Reap

 09 Retro Kampot Guesthouse, Kampot

10 Firefly Guesthouse, Koh Rong

INTRODUCTION TO CAMBODIA

Your Cambodia Bucket List

Drink Each Of The Following Once...
○ Anchor Beer
○ Angkor Beer
○ Cambodia Beer
○ Fresh Coconut
○ Sugar Cane Juice
○ Joss Shot

Eat Each Of The Following Once...
○ Nhoam Krauch Thlong: Pomelo Salad
○ Nhoam Svay Kchai: Green Mango Salad
○ Amok: A Curry Best with Fish or Chicken
○ Kari Saraman: Beef Curry
○ Fresh Fruit Smoothie
○ Durian

Do Each Of The Following Once...
○ Get a Massage
○ Order Dinner Speaking in Khmer
○ Ride in a Tuk Tuk
○ Eat a Bug
○ Swim in the Ocean
○ Ride in a Longtail Boat
○ Sleep in Floating Bungalows
○ Watch the Sunset on the Beach
○ Have Cocktails with a New Friend

CAMBODIA
Survival Guide

Quick Things to Consider..............23
Weather in Cambodia.....................24
The Voltage in Cambodia..............25
Tourist Visas for Cambodia...........26
What to Pack for Cambodia..........30
How to Budget for Cambodia.......34
Internet and Data in Cambodia.....40
Khmer Language Guide.................42
Transportation in Cambodia.........46
Safe Girl Tips & Advice.................52
Crime & Safety in Cambodia........52
Safety Tips for Cambodia..............54
Do's & Dont's...................................56
Activities to Avoid.........................58

SURVIVAL GUIDE

Quick Things to Consider

HOW LONG DO YOU NEED?

The ideal amount of time to come to Cambodia is 1-2 months.

2 months is immersive, 1 month is comprehensive and 2 weeks is rushed, but you can do it.

VISAS

You do not need to apply for a tourist visa ahead of time, but you can, and you can stay up to two months (1 month visa + 1 month extension).

MONEY

Cambodia uses US dollars and Cambodian Riel. So feel free to bring a stack of $10 bills in USD (anything bigger is hard to break).

BACKPACKS ONLY

Don't even think about bringing a rolley suitcase on these streets.

COVID PROTOCOL

Rules change all the time. But at the time of this publication, vaccinated travelers can enter Cambodia with proof of vaccination. No PCR test needed.

SURVIVAL GUIDE

Weather in Cambodia

The Good News: Weather patterns are easily predictable with 2 whole seasons per year.

The Bad News: It's humid and sticky no matter what.

When planning your epic Cambodian adventure, keep these two seasons in mind as they can be the make or break for a lot of activities…

Dry Season runs from late October to April. This is the season with the least rain. Come November – January, and you'll experience the pleasant temperatures in the high 60s. However, after January, the temperatures start to heat up. April is usually boiling with temps that reach over 100 °.

Green Season lasts from May to October with monsoons bringing lots of rainfall. The beginning of Wet Season (May to July) is relatively cool with temps ranging from 75° to 80° and rain falling only a couple hours per day.

The second half of the rainy season (August-October), however, is no stranger to full days of non-stop rain. With Cambodia's underdeveloped roads and limited septic systems, expect travel delays with flooded roads and flooded septic tanks. It's not exactly barefoot beach weather, ya know

These weather patterns correspond to the tourist industry's High Season and Low Season. Each season has its perks and pitfalls.

The Low Season *(May-September)* sees a lower volume of tourists due to the rain. While you won't get an amazing tan during this time period, you will get discounted hotel prices and flights! You'll also experience lush green jungles and unobstructed photo ops at Angkor Wat.

The High Season (*November to February*) has the most gorgeous weather that is best for beach days and flip flops! Weather will not be getting in your way, but the larger flocks of tourists might. Expect social beaches and full-priced flights. If you're a people person or a bargain hunter, you might enjoy this challenge.

So to sum all of that up...

Hottest Months	May-June 95 °F / 35 °C and hotter
Coolest Months	November-December 75 °F /24 °C with a breeze
Most Humid Months	March-April
Most Popular Time to Visit	November- February or "High Season"
Alexa's Favorite Time to Visit:	November - June

THE VOLTAGE IN CAMBODIA

The voltage in Cambodia is 230V and 50Hz. Translation: if you're from the US or UK, your curling iron and hair dryer won't work here but your basic electronics will be fine!

For electric outlets, you'll commonly see Type A and Type C sockets like this.

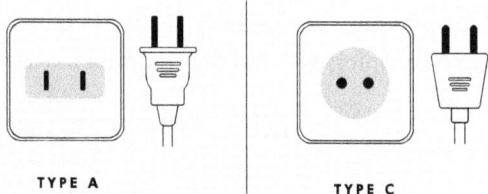

TYPE A   TYPE C

Unless you're carrying sensitive electronics (like said hair dryer) you won't need an international adapter which converts the actual voltage. You'll just need a plug adapter, like this one. ☞

SURVIVAL GUIDE

SURVIVAL GUIDE

Tourist Visa for Cambodia

How long can you actually stay in Cambodia?

Stay in Cambodia for 30 - 60 Days

Here's the deal: Tourists are allowed to enter and explore Cambodia for 30 days on arrival.

You can extend this for an extra 30 days = 60 days total in Cambodia.

To extend, any hostel or hotel can help you do this. They will take your passport for a few days, don't freak out. They do this all the time.

Want to stay longer than 60 days?

Do a "visa run". This is where you visit a nearby country like Vietnam, Thailand, or Laos for a few days to reset your visa, and then you enter back into the country on a new visa.

*Immigration starts to get suspicious once you've done this 3 or 4 times back to back - they know what you're doing now and they may not like it.

PRO TIP! No, you can't drink the tap water—but it is safe to brush your teeth and bathe in!

HOW TO GET YOUR TOURIST VISA

01 Visa on Arrival

Just show up. When you land in Cambodia or cross over into Cambodia on land, you apply for your visa then. No steps or paperwork to file before you come to Cambodia.

What you need:

→ 2 Passport Photos

→ $30 US Cash

→ 1 Full Blank Page in your Passport

→ Application Form (that you receive and fill out at immigration when you land)

→ There are many visa options on the Application Form. You want to check the T Visa.

01 The Online e-Visa

You can apply online for your visa before you come to Cambodia. This will save you time in lines (at least, hypothetically). Print out your form and bring it with you to immigration along with two passport photos.

Here's how to apply online:

○ **Step 1:** Go to the e-Visa webpage: www.evisa.gov.kh

○ **Step 2:** Fill in the application

○ **Step 3:** Pay the fee or $30 USD plus $6 for the service fee

○ **Step 4:** Wait for visa approval. You'll get an email with your visa within 3 business days.

○ **Step 5:** Print your visa and present it at immigration in Cambodia.

IMPORTANT NOTE: The e-Visa is only accepted at Siem Reap and Phnom Penh airports, Koh Kong & Poipet Border Crossing (from Thailand), and Bavet Border Crossing (from Vietnam).

If you have questions about staying in Cambodia long term, join this Facebook Group:

Cambodia Visa and Work Permit Group ☞

WHAT TO EXPECT AT IMMIGRATION

Airport Immigration is smooth. You get off the plane, walk up to the immigration desk, hand them all your documents with your passport and wait about 10-30 minutes for your visa to be put in your passport. Then you go through the official immigration line and viola! – Welcome to Cambodia!

At least, that's airport immigration.

Border Immigration (crossing over land via Thailand, Laos or Vietnam), however, requires patience.

When leaving Thailand, Laos, or Vietnam – there are two immigration points for you to cross.

○ **Immigration Point #1:** You will officially exit the country by visiting that country's immigration checkpoint where you'll receive your exit stamp.

○ **Immigration Point #2:** Then, you'll then walk through a strange 'no man's land' between the two countries. Just follow the people. You can't mess this up. You will then arrive at Cambodia's border, collect an application form, fill it out and then stand in line to receive your visa.

⚠ **BEWARE:** You might be approached by porters that speak incredible English, offer to carry your bag and help you with the visa process. For a $5 fee, of course. When the lines are super long with lots of travelers, I see no harm in slipping a dude some cash to skip the line for you.

⚠ ⚠ **BEWARE AGAIN:** Tuk Tuk drivers will sometimes tell you that you need to go to the "Visa Office" first to apply for your visa. Usually this "office" is near the border where they charge you some bogus fee for a bogus service.

Listen love, the only thing you need to do is get your exit stamp from the official immigration counter and walk to the next immigration point. If a Tuk Tuk tries to take advantage of the situation and take you to the visa office, just tell them that you already have a visa and stay in the Tuk Tuk (even if you don't).

NERVOUS?

Even I get nervous before (and during) a new trip. The secret? Turn that nervous energy into excited energy. Instead of saying "I'm afraid to do this" say "I can't wait to do this" and let life happen.

Wanna become a pro traveler?
Join The Solo Girl's Travel Academy ☞

SURVIVAL GUIDE

What to Pack for Cambodia

I always say, as long as you have your passport, bank card and a decent backpack, you're ready to travel Southeast Asia. Most things that you need or forget at home can be purchased here, just at a slightly more expensive price.

So, let's get organized now. It's taken me years to perfect packing for Asia, but I've finally got it down. This list will teach you in 3 minutes what I learned in 5 years.

WHAT TO PACK

✓ PASSPORT WITH AT LEAST 6 MONTHS VALIDITY

Some countries enforce it and some countries don't – but to play it safe, you need to have at least 6 months validity on your passport. For example, if it's January 1st, 2024, and your passport expires before June 1st, 2024, they might not let you in the country and you'll have to return home immediately.

✓ TRAVEL INSURANCE

Yes, you do need it. Everything from minor bouts of food poisoning to helicopter medevac off a mountain, a standard travel insurance policy is a non-negotiable in my (literal) book. Check your current medical insurance plan. They might already cover Thailand. If they don't, here is what I use:

  ✈ **World Nomads** which offers full-coverage plans for extremely reasonable prices.

✈ **SafetyWing** is also a really affordable option, especially if you're traveling long term.

✓ THE PERFECT BACKPACK OR SUITCASE

The Bag I Recommend…

The Osprey Farpoint 40 Litre Backpack ☞

It's been over 5 years that I've been using this bag. I love it so much that I just bought the exact same model again to use for another 5 years.

♥ This bag qualifies as a carry-on

♥ It's extremely comfortable to wear

♥ The open-zip style means that you can keep your clothes organized

♥ I swear it's got Mary Poppins magic because I can fit 3 months of clothes in one tiny space

 Or the **Osprey Fairview 55** that comes with a zip-on and off day bag.

✓ WALKING SHOES

Bring 3 pairs of shoes:

◊ 1 Pair of Flip Flops or Slides

◊ 1 Pair of Cute Walking Sandals

◊ 1 Pair of Hiking / Running Shoes

This is my official trifecta of shoes. Through rain, up mountains, and on long sweaty walks, they've never failed me. I replace the same pairs of shoes every year – find them in my travel store.

✓ A SHAWL

For cold bus rides and modest temples, you'll find yourself grabbing your shawl or scarf often. Don't have one? Consider buying a beautiful handmade shawl at one of the markets here.

✓ OB TAMPONS OR A MENSTRUAL CUP

You're going to be in a bathing suit on the beach and out on the water! And if you've never used a menstrual cup, they are a game changer. Save money every month, go 12 hours with no leaks & swim with no drips.

I use the Saalt Cup and my life has changed forever.

✓ ELECTRIC ADAPTER

It's not just the socket you have to worry about, it's also the voltage. Your phone and laptop are likely not going to be compatible with the Thai outlets. REI, Target, and Amazon have cheap Universal adapters that every traveler should own.

✓ QUICK DRY TOWEL

Hostel girls! Hostels usually don't provide towels so it's nice to bring a travel towel of your own. Not a total necessity, but a quick dry (usually some kind of microfiber) towel is nice to have– especially during the rainy season when the heat isn't there to dry things quickly. Plus, it can double as your beach towel!

✓ TROPICAL WEATHER MAKEUP

Humidity is no joke. Most foundations get super greasy and eyeshadows crease like it's their job. My makeup bag is pure perfection when it comes to long-lasting, humid, tropical weather products. Check out my travel makeup collection here.

✓ MONEY CONCEAL POUCH

This credit card size pouch is used to discreetly carry cash, cards, and keys. The Velcro strap makes it easy to secure the pouch to your bra or undies

✓ EMERGENCY MONEY SOURCE / $100 CASH US

Have a secret stash of cash and a backup credit card in case you get in a sticky situation. Keep this emergency money source separate from your other cards and cash so that if you lose your wallet, you won't lose the secret stash, too

✓ BANK CARDS

Travel with two cards – either 2 debit cards or 1 debit + 1 credit. In the case that your bank flags one card with fraudulent activity and disables it, you'll want to have a backup. If the machine eats a card, if a card gets stolen, or if you lose your purse on a night out, a backup card will make all the difference between having mom fly you home and you continuing your travels.

The cards you need are here. ☞

NOTE! If you are from the UK, check out Starling Bank. They have the best atm exchange rates and don't charge any foreign atm charges. They can also send you a replacement if you lose or break your card to anywhere in the world that has an address!

✓ EMPTY SPACE IN YOUR BAG

It took me 5 years to learn that the less stuff you have, the more free you are. You are free to pick up and move around, free to shop for souvenirs, and free from relying on porters and taxis to help you carry your luggage.

WHAT NOT TO PACK

- ✗ Jeans
- ✗ High-heels
- ✗ Hairspray (ya won't use it)
- ✗ A Curling Iron (with this humidity…no point)
- ✗ Too Many Bras (ya won't wear em')
- ✗ A Pharmacy of Medicine (you can get it all here)

SURVIVAL GUIDE

How to Budget for Cambodia

How much money should I bring?
How much will I spend? What is the least amount I can spend and still see it all?

When it comes to traveling Southeast Asia, there are 3 spending routes you can take:

Budget 💵

Stay in hostels, eat local, take the super convenient minibus, and drink beer from 7-Eleven.

Balanced 💵 💵

Spend the night in a hostel and eat street food one night, then check into a beachfront resort and sip tropical cocktails the next. Or just stay middle of the road the whole way through—not too fancy but comfortable.

Bougie 💵 💵 💵

Infinity pool resorts, private boat tours, and quick flights from one beach to the next.

	BUDGET	BALANCED	BOUGIE
TOTAL PER DAY	$30	$80	$160+

All 3 of these options are possible, easy and will offer you the trip of a lifetime—as long as you plan it right.

— DAILY EXPENSES —

Street Food	$1.50
Restaurant	$4.00
Hamburger	$8.00
Bottle of Beer	$3.00
Cocktail	$5.00
1 Night in a Hostel	$8.00
1 Night in a Private Room	$30.00
1 Night in a Resort	$110.00+
Day Tour	$30
1 Hour Flight	$25–150
7 hour Bus	$28

MONEY HACKS

💰 Use ATMs Sparingly

ATM fees are high in Cambodia. You can spend $6-$12 withdrawing cash!

Only visit the ATM once a week, take out the cash you'll need, and don't carry it all around with you! Stash it in your backpack and lock your backpack.

💰 Avoid Fees - Use a Debit Card with No Foreign Transaction Fee

This will literally save you hundreds of dollars! A debit card with no foreign transaction fee will reimburse you for all the transaction fees you've been charged at an ATM.

I use the Charles Schwab Brokerage Debit card.

⚜ Use your Credit Card

Many hotels and restaurants (but not all) accept credit cards. You can also use websites like 12go.asia to book your transportation and avoid paying cash.

You can learn more about the cards I travel with here ☞

⚜ Use ATMs inside Convenience Stores

As a universal travel rule, ATMs inside supermarkets, convenient stores, and banks are your biggest insurance policies against you becoming a victim of fraud or having a wad of cash ripped out of your hand.

⚜ Bring US Dollars

Cambodia uses two currencies: the US Dollar and the Cambodian Riel. You can use them interchangeably.

⚜ Learn to Count Riel

Let's say you buy a beer with a $10 US bill. It's likely that you'll get your change in Riel.

So now you have both USD and Riel in your wallet - what the hell are you supposed to do with that?

I like to think of USD as my real money and Riel as the paper version of spare change or coins. It's not uncommon to pay for something that costs $5.50 with a $5 US bill and 2,000 khr

⚜ Carry Small Bills

Tuk Tuk drivers can't (or will pretend like they can't) break a $10 or $20 in USD. Always have $5 and $1 bills on you.

KNOW BEFORE YOU GO

The bills come in the following denominations and here are their approximate round-up values:

→ 1,000 = .25 cents
→ 5,000 khr = $1.22 USD
→ 10,000 khr = $2.50 USD
→ 20,000 khr = $5 USD
→ 50,000 khr = $12 USD
→ 100,000 khr = $25 USD

PRO TIP! Know your money colors...

Each bill has a unique color, unlike the US dollar. Familiarize yourself with these colors to make sure you don't mistakenly hand over a 10,000 when you mean to hand over a 1,000!

- 1,000 is blue and purple
- 5,000 is brown and violet
- 10,000 is blue and brown
- 20,000 is orange and pink
- 50,000 is brown and yellow
- 100,000 is green

CAMBODIAOFFICIALPAGE.BLOGSPOT.COM

Tips to Spend Less in Cambodia

✔ Visit during "low season" when accommodation and flights are cheaper

✔ Get a Sim Card to download Grab Taxi or Pass App

✔ Drink beer from hole in the wall bars, rather than clubs

✔ Haggle at markets and when street shopping! Start haggling at half price and work your way from there.

✔ Use tuk tuk drivers only when necessary

Your biggest expenses will be

- Alcohol
- Partying
- Organized Island Tours

Everything else can be tweaked to fit your wallet.

CARDS YOU SHOULD BE TRAVELING WITH ESPECIALLY IF YOU'RE COMING TO ASIA LONG-TERM

My # 1 Travel Rule: Don't book your flight and hotels with a debit card!

☞ **Reason #1:** If your flight or trip is cancelled, you will have no trip protection and you may never see your cash again.

☞ **Reason #2:** You are literally turning down free money if you're not taking advantage of travel credit card points when booking international flights and weeks of hotels.

Use a Travel Credit Card to…

◊ Book your flight

◊ Book your hotels

◊ Pay at restaurants

What About Debit Cards?

FOR AMERICANS, open an account with Charles Schwab Bank. With Charles Schwab, I can use any ATM in the world without ATM fees. Every time you use an ATM that isn't your bank's ATM, you are charged a "foreign ATM fee" that can be $3–8 depending on where you are. Lame. But at the end of every month, Charles Schwab reimburses all foreign ATM fees.

Chase and American Express are the cards I can't live without. I explain why I love these cards here:

HEY! WANT TO TRAVEL WITH ME?

CHECK OUT GLOWUPTRAVEL.COM

SURVIVAL GUIDE

Internet & Data in Cambodia

While the internet around Cambodia isn't too reliable, data plans are! With service available on remote islands, 4G is a lifesaver. I use two companies: 'Smart' and 'Metfone'- they've got the most comprehensive coverage around the country. SIM Cards are available starting at $5 USD. You can find a kiosk outside any airport…or literally everywhere in town. Cambodians love their data plans.

FUN FACT: South East Asians are the #1 consumer of phone data in the world.

No, **don't get an "international plan" with your cell phone carrier from home** (unless it's GoogleFi). Your coverage will be shit and 10x more expensive. This goes for Thailand, Cambodia, Vietnam and Bali…everywhere in Asia.

I use AIS and I pay around $15 USD per month.

▣ PHONE PRO TIP:
When calling from outside of Cambodia with an international number (anything other than Cambodian), add the country code (+855) and make sure you've dropped the first 0. When calling with a Cambodian number, drop the country code and add a 0.

For example: +855 23 427 124 = 023 427 124

Same number. Different input.

DOWNLOAD LOCAL APPS

Cambodia is connected to some awesome apps that will make your trip a lot easier and a lot cheaper if you use them!

GrabTaxi, WeGo and PassApp

These are like Uber but cheaper. You can order cars, tuk tuks and motorbikes. You can pay cash on the taxi meter or connect your debit card to the app.

Line Messenger App

The messenger app that most Khmer locals use in place of texting. This app works on WIFI and data for both calling and texting.

WhatsApp

But also download Whatsapp. Most travelers and expats use this free messaging app to talk to each other.

GoogleMaps Offline

You can save Google's Cambodia-map offline, so that even when you don't have access to Wi-Fi or data, you can still navigate.

TripIt

Whenever you get an email confirmation from flight, hotel, or tour – forward the flight to Travefy which will organize your itinerary on your phone. Now you have your booking confirmations, flight times, address, and maps in one place!

Bumble And Tinder

Link up with a local who knows all the best spots in the city or find a sightseeing partner with another traveler. Cambodia is very pro-dating app. **Fun Fact:** Bumble has a friend-mode called Bumble BFF where you can search for new friends to explore with!

XE

Currency Conversions in an instant

MY FACEBOOK GROUPS TO JOIN

 The Solo Girl's Travel Community
where you can ask questions and meet other girls.

The Solo Girl's Travel Guide
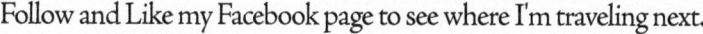
Follow and Like my Facebook page to see where I'm traveling next.

SURVIVAL GUIDE

Khmer Language Guide

The local language is called **"Khmer"** – pronounced *"Ka-My."*

Many Cambodians, especially the younger generation in the areas most frequented by travelers, speak decent English. But you will undoubtedly need to communicate with Cambodians who don't speak English.

The good news about Khmer is that it isn't tonal. It's phonetic. Which means that the words sound just like they're spelled. This is an easy language to learn. Let's try.

GREETINGS

Hello	Sus-a-dei
How are you?	Soks-a-bye
I'm fine	Soks-a-bye (the same as above)
What's your name?	Cham-moo-ey
My name is...	Knyom-cham-moo
Sorry / Excuse me	Som-toe
Good-bye	Lee hi
Thank-you	Akun

DAY TO DAY

Yes (for women)	Bah
Yes (for men)	Chaa
No	Ot Tey

I don't know	Knyom mung dan te
I don't understand	Knyom mung yul te
Where's the toilet?	Bung kun new-a-nah

SHOPPING

How much?	Bow-man
I want one	Khnyom chong-ban moi
I don't want	Khnyom min chong-ban moi
Too expensive	T-Lay

NUMBERS

1	Moi
2	Bee
3	Bai
4	Boum
5	Bram
6	Bram moi
7	Bram bee
8	Bram bai
9	Bram boun
19	Dop

PRO TIP! Want to learn more Khmer?

Download the app Simply Learn Khmer and start practicing.

FOOD

I'm hungry	K-noym-kleam
Delicious	ch-nang
Water, please	Som tach
Beer	Sra beer
Cocktail	Sra krolok
Spicy	Hul
Don't want spicy	Ming chon hul
Noodles	Mi
Coffee	Cafe
Rice	Bay
Chicken	Sak mon
Pork	Sak chrou
Beef	Sak ko
Shrimp	Bang-kea
Fish	Trei
Coconut	Daung
Fruit	Ply-cheu
Banana	Chek
Check, please	Ket loy

DIRECTIONS

Go straight	Da-trong
Turn left	Baht schweng

Turn right	Baht saddam
Here	Tini
Stop	Chop

EMERGENCY PHRASES

Help!	Chouy
Police	Police
Thief	Cha-ow

TRAVEL NOTES:

....

....

....

....

....

....

♥ **Want to see how I travel Cambodia?**

Check out my Cambodia Highlight on Instagram @sologirlstravelguide

SURVIVAL GUIDE

Transporation in Cambodia

Cambodia is relatively new to the tourism industry - that's what makes it such an exciting destination!

However, this also means that some destinations are still a bit choppy in terms of traveling from Point A to Point B.

For the destinations that have their shit together (Phnom Penh, Siem Reap, Battambang, etc.), getting there is as easy as asking your hotel to book a bus or a minivan – and your transportation will pick you up directly from your hotel.

When it comes to islands, border crossings and off the beaten path destinations, however, you'll need a little extra help. For these destinations, I've added some extra insider advice to get you there safely, quickly, and without spending all your cash!

Throughout this Cambodia Guide, you'll occasionally come across the extra "How to Get There" section at the end of various chapters. These are the cheat codes and travel hacks to make your journey smoother.

But in general, here's what you need to know about getting around Cambodia.

The main highlights in Cambodia are spread out from north to south - but getting between them is easy! Choosing your mode of transportation depends on your budget.

For example: Siem Reap to Phnom Penh
- → 7 hours by bus - $9-$12 USD
- → 5 hours by private taxi - $75 USD
- → 55 minutes by air - $100 USD

I use 12go.asia to check my options and when convenient, book my transport.

Besides cost, here are some things to help you navigate your route.

BY BUS

For backpackers, this is the number one way to travel. Depending on the route, some buses are filled with backpackers making the ride feel like a mini summer camp. But there are some things you need to know about bus life in Cambodia.

Riding the local Cambodian buses is not ideal.

Remember, Cambodia is a developing country. There are little safety regulations enforced upon public transport. Buses breakdown, staff can be sketchy, drivers are overworked and often fall asleep at the wheel or take amphetamines to stay awake.

Instead, here are a list of companies I trust:

Giant Ibis

Giant Ibis has self-imposed safety standards and professional training for their staff. For long distance rides, Giant Ibis hires 2 drivers who switch positions when the other gets sleepy. Plus, they are air conditioned, provide water and snacks, and have electric sockets onboard. I promote Giant Ibis as often as I can. I don't work for them or get any commission. I just trust them with my life.

Other Companies I like:
- → **Mekong Express**
- → **Cambodia Post VIP**
- → **Larryta Express**
- → **Bayon VIP**
- → **Seila Angkor**

🌐 ***Book at:***

I use 12go.asia to book my transport for just about everything.

But if I'm staying at a hostel or a guest house, it's also convenient to book through them.

BY TAXI

I love sitting in a private taxi, staring out the window as we pass through villages and countryside - stopping for snacks along the way.

When you're traveling with 2 - 4 people, this is absolutely the most budget-friendly and convenient way to travel.

PRO TIP WHEN HIRING A LONG DISTANCE TAXI DRIVER…

The faster they drive, the more money they can squeeze into a day. Makes sense. BUT these fast driving taxis are not invincible to road accidents. I always offer my drivers an extra $5 to drive slower. "How long does the trip take? 3 hours. Ok, I'll pay you an extra $5 if you make it 3.5 hours."

When the trip is $40 for a 4 hour ride, that extra $5 is a fair incentive to slow down. And then you can feel justified if you feel compelled to ask the driver to slow down along your journey.

At the end of this guide, you'll find my Driver Directory with a list of drivers I trust.

Want to Share a Taxi?

Taxi rides can be more comfortable than minivan rides and faster than bus rides. Sharing taxis is a common thing here in Cambodia! It's convenient and also a great way to meet new people. Before you travel in-between cities…

☞ Check out the Facebook group Taxi Share Cambodia. There may be someone offering a Taxi share or you can suggest one.

☞ Or ask the reception at your hotel or hostel if you can post a Taxi Sign Up Sheet with your trip details.

<u>BY TRAIN</u>

Old rickety trains that pass through forests and small towns are such a peaceful way to travel like a local. Here are some train routes to consider:

Phnom Penh to Kampot

🕐 *How long:* 3 hours

💵 *How Much:* $9 USD

🕐 *When:* Daily at 7am from Phnom Penh Railway Station

🌐 *Book at:* royalrailway.easybook.com

Phnom Penh to Sihanoukville

This is the same train as above - Sihanoukville is the next stop

🕐 *How long:* 3.5 hours

💵 *How Much:* $10 USD

🕐 *When:* Daily at 7am from Phnom Penh Railway Station

🌐 *Book at:* royalrailway.easybook.com

Phnom Penh to Battambang

⊙ *How long:* 8 hours

💰 *How Much:* $10 USD

⊙ *When:* Daily at 6:40am from Phnom Penh Railway Station

🌐 *Book at:* royalrailway.easybook.com

BY TUK TUK

Tuk Tuk drivers are hustlers and you can't blame them. Always haggle.

Tuk Tuks are usually used for quick rides in town and sometimes, depending on the location, from the airport into town.

Rides range from $1-$15 depending on the distance.

MOTORBIKES

If you're comfortable on a motorbike, they can be a great way to get off the beaten path and explore solo. But here are the rules to follow:

✓ Always wear a helmet.

✓ Keep your purse under the seat compartment or under your clothing while you ride, especially at night. Thieves have been known to try and steal your bag while riding.

✓ Never ever ever drive drunk.

✓ Take photos of the bike before you ride away with it. Take photos of any scratches or damages so that you're not blamed for them.

✓ Take a photo of your license plate in case you lose your bike in a parking lot.

✔ Take pictures of the motorbike before you rent it. Take photos of any scratches or damages so you won't be held liable. Take a photo of the license plate, too, so you don't lose it!

✔ American? Go to AAA to get an international drivers' license for $20. No test. Just your passport, 2 passport photos and 20- minutes needed.

✔ Also also, if the Police catch you driving without an international drivers' license (not a common occurrence), they may ask for a bribe. Try to convince them that you only have 10,000 riel. They'll eventually accept it and let you leave.

SURVIVAL GUIDE: SAFE GIRL TIPS

Safe Girl Tips & Advice

CRIME & SAFETY IN CAMBODIA

Your life is not in danger, but your wallet certainly may be.

Crime in Cambodia typically comes in the form of scams and theft. Each city varies in terms of what scams are run and which methods are used by thieves to target foreigners. Let's get into it….

Milk Scams

Female beggars will approach you, usually with a baby, and ask you to buy powdered milk to feed their baby. You'll go with them to a shop and buy the milk – thinking that you've done a low risk good deed since no cash was exchanged. Not so fast. Sadly, the mothers are working with the shopkeepers. The shopkeepers take back the milk and a cut of the money, while the mothers keep the rest of the cash.

📍 **Where:** These scams are most popular in Siem Reap.

❓ **What to do:** Beggars lose interest easily when they see that you're not interested. Say 'no' once and then don't make eye contact. It's a sucky feeling…but you can solve the entire problem in one night.

Landmines

It is estimated that there are 4-6 million unexploded landmines in Cambodia which are left over from the Vietnam war.

⚑ Where: With its unexplored jungles and protected Angkor Wat empire, there is a lot of land left untouched in the north of Cambodia.

❷ What to do: Don't stray from the paths around Angkor Wat, in the jungle or in rural areas and farmland.

Thieves on Motorbikes

Motorbikes will drive by and snatch your purse or jewelry right off of your body. They will also take your phone right from your hands. Tuk Tuks are not a safe zone either. Thieves will reach into a Tuk Tuk and grab your bags that are lying on the floor. Thieves are ruthless and are not afraid to cause injury.

⚑ Where: This crime is prominent in Phnom Penh and Sihanoukville. Incidents in Kampot are also on the rise.

❷ What to do: Avoid walking at night. If you must walk…don't carry a purse or bag at all. Spend the extra $3 to take a Tuk Tuk back to your hotel and if you're in Phnom Penh, use the driving service called PassApp (kind of like Uber but with a Rickshaw!).

AN ANECDOTAL STORY FOR YOU...

One night, in Phnom Penh, I was walking home from a bar with 2 friends: 1 small girl and 1 very tall guy. We noticed two motorbikes following us, passing us and then turning back around. Circling us. They were waiting for the right opportunity to drive up next to us and grab our purses. Our guy friend confronted them with a "Hey, we see what you're trying to do" and they eventually gave up. Lesson: Make eye contact, confront the idiots, and always be on guard no matter how many people are in your group. Don't be afraid to yell.

Motorbikes and Car Crashes

Man oh man. There are far too many traffic accidents in Cambodia. You have monster 16-wheel trucks next to tiny motorbikes passing each other on dirt roads. You have cows on the road. You have drunk drivers galore.

♥ **Where:** Everywhere

❂ **What to do:** Always wear your seatbelt in a car and always secure your helmet tightly when riding a motorbike. Don't ride or drive with someone you have an uneasy feeling about. Practice riding your motorbike in rural areas before driving in the city or on main roads before you start driving yourself

SAFETY TIPS FOR CAMBODIA

♥ Wear a Cross Shoulder Purse

This certainly makes it more difficult for thieves to remove your bag from your body. Also make sure the straps of the bag are relatively thick and aren't easy to cut.

♥ Look Both Ways Before you Cross the Street

Duh, but really- traffic here is different than back home. Pedestrians don't have the right of way here- even on a green light. When crossing the street, don't just look for cars- look for motorbikes that whiz between the cars, too!

♥ Let's Talk about Sexual Assault

Foreign women (that's us) are statistically more likely to be sexually assaulted by a foreign man (other travelers) on vacation than they are to be sexually assaulted by a Khmer man. Think about it; in hostels, hotels and bars- we are more likely to be hanging around foreign men, quite possibly with alcohol in our systems, and therefore exposed to that risk. Just like you would at home, monitor your sobriety levels and be aware of your surroundings.

♥ Protect your Phone

While on the street, text on your phone like you would when you're not supposed to be texting in class. Don't hold your phone out in front of you while texting or ordering a PassApp. Also, don't leave your phone sitting on the table at a restaurant. It may disappear.

PRO TIP: Get a solid phone case with a phone grip from OtterBox before you have a wild adventure and lose your phone with all your photos.

Get it here:

♥ Put your Bags Behind your Body in a Tuk Tuk

Conceal your bags and make them difficult to grab. Thieves like convenience.

♥ Be So Careful Walking at Night

Make smart choices. Stay on lit roads, walk with a friend, and don't get super drunk and wander off by yourself. All of the above will make you a target very quickly.

<u>Areas that are Relatively Safe to Walk at Night:</u>

📍 **The Riverside in Phnom Penh:** I've only had lovely experiences here – but I am aware that little thieves are waiting for someone to set their purse down. Just keep an eye out while you stroll along the river in the evening (before 9 or 10pm).

📍 **Serendipity Road and Beach in Sihanoukville:** I personally know women who have been victims of motorbike thieves in Sihanoukville, but not directly on Serendipity Road. You do need to watch your purse very carefully on the beach, however. My purse was stolen while I had it sitting next to me in a beach chair - I didn't even notice (the full story is at the end of this book).

📍 **The Night Market in Siem Reap:** This area doesn't see too much crime.

📍 **All of Koh Rong:** The islands never sleep so you don't get a "seedy" time of night. That being said, don't get too carefree with your belongings on a night out. I remember a friend left their Kindle in the bathroom for 2 minutes and it was swiped. Keep your bag and valuables on your body. If you set it down, someone else will pick it up.

DO'S & DONT'S FOR CAMBODIA

Here's a quick list of cultural and local norms to make you feel more comfortable from the start.

DO

♥ Haggle

Aside from restaurants and food stalls, you can pretty much haggle any price in Cambodia. Tuk Tuk drivers, taxi drivers, street market vendors, clothing stalls…every price is negotiable especially when you're buying more than one dress or are traveling with more than one person in a tuk tuk. Worst case, they don't budge.

♥ Cover your Shoulders & Knees in Temples

Modesty is required inside spiritual spaces. Wear a long skirt, or buy a beautiful shawl to wrap around your waist and/or shoulders when you visit the temples.

♥ Tip Your Salon Lady

Massages, pedicures, haircuts- these kinds of services definitely deserve a tip. 15-20% should do it.

♥ Conceal your Cell Phone

Instead of leaving your cell phone sitting on your table or casually texting in public, keep it protected or hidden.

♥ Get a Walking Beer

When in Rome! There are no 'open carry' laws here so feel free to crack open a cold one as you peruse the night markets or walk along the beach.

♥ Refer to Cambodians as Khmers

You'll hear this word a lot. Khmer (Ka-Mair) people speak Khmer (Ka-My) language. The same spelling but a different pronunciation. Now you know!

DON'T

✗ Wear Bikinis in Public

I know you're on vacation, but the locals are not. You wouldn't walk through a stranger's living room in your thong, so why would you walk through their village in your bikini? Save your banging bod for the beach or the pool and cover up while you walk around town.

✗ Tip Taxis or Servers

I mean, you can if you want to. But typically, Khmers don't tip. In some situations, tipping is actually quite awkward.

✗ Touch a Monk

No one, not me, not you, not Oprah, can touch a monk. No handshakes, no selfies, and no hugs.

✗ Walk Alone at Night

In recent years, Cambodia has seen a spike in petty theft. In Phnom Penh, be aware of Cambodians on motorbikes that wait to follow you and grab your purse. It's best not to carry a purse at all.

ACTIVITIES TO AVOID

You don't know what you don't know. Here's some quick insight into responsible tourism in The Bode.

Volunteering at an Orphanage

<u>**A rule of thumb for Cambodia:**</u> If an organization allows strangers to come and play with their children, then this organization does not have the children's best intentions at heart.

The "volun-tourism" industry in Cambodia is booming. Kind-hearted tourists and travelers visit Cambodia with good intentions set on helping disadvantaged children, women, and youth.

Knowing that, there is essentially a market for kind hearts, dark and twisted "charities" and "orphanages" have been popping up all over the third and developing world. These organizations pose as orphanages, filling their beds with children who have literally been rented from their families, but are nothing more than money-making schemes. In fact, the standard estimate is that 70% of these children have at least 1 parent who is alive and capable of care. These children are not orphans, they are rented props living in Child Zoos.

So, while you believe that you are teaching English, helping the orphanage build a well, or spending time with abandoned babies…what is actually happening is that you are feeding an industry that exploits children for profit.

You must be very very careful when choosing where to volunteer. As a rule of thumb, avoid ANY organization that offers you the chance to "play with the kids."

If you still want to volunteer, there is a respected and transparent organization called CHOICE which provides resources to Cambodia's poorest communities. When you volunteer with CHOICE, you'll join in on a village trip where you'll collect water and food and then deliver these resources to villages in need.

There will not be any Facebook photos or opportunities to play with the kids. Instead, you'll contribute in a sustainable and impactful way with a $15 donation to the organization and leave with an insight into the true status of poverty in South East Asia and what the world can do to help.

For more volunteer opportunities, check out the Volunteer Section for some fabulous volunteer opportunities around Cambodia!

Getting Tattoos of Buddha

Buddha is sacred in these parts. So much so that in nearby Myanmar, a backpacker was once jailed for having a tattoo of Buddha. That is quite unlikely to happen to you in Cambodia, but it goes to show how disrespectful it is.

Riding Elephants

What may seem like a 'Bucket List' activity is actually an industry bred out of animal cruelty and torture. Instead of riding elephants, find an elephant sanctuary that allows you to feed, trek and bathe in the river with elephants rescued from the circus, work camps and elephant riding tourist centers around Cambodia. Check out the elephant sanctuary, EVP, in Mondulkiri or visit nearby Cambodia which has plenty of amazing Elephant Sanctuaries throughout the country. Check out the Cambodia section of this book for more info.

Visiting Tiger Temples

Those cute baby tigers that you're about to take a photo with...do you ever wonder where they come from? Tigers are essentially farmed, taken from their mothers at 2 weeks old, and given to tourists to bottle feed. And that's only the beginning...

CHAPTER ONE

Phnom Penh

📷 @NOAH4EVER

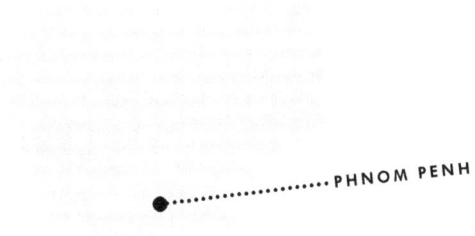

CHAPTER ONE

Phnom Penh

To understand Phnom Penh, you need to understand its history.

On April 17, 1975, a vicious military guerilla group led by heinous leader Pol Pot, drove tanks through the streets of Phnom Penh and began a reign of terror over the country. First, they removed families from their homes, separated children from their parents, turned kids into gun wielding-soldiers, and filled up labor camps around the country.

This military guerilla group, The Khmer Rouge, specifically targeted doctors, lawyers, artists, teachers and intellectuals- anyone who could think for themselves and possibly revolt. These people were murdered.

The Khmer Rouge was in power for just 4 years. By the time the regime fell in 1979, over 2 million people had been murdered. That was only 40 years ago. Today, Cambodia is in the middle of rebuilding their infrastructure, culture, and government from the ground up. What you'll experience when you visit Phnom Penh- the former epicenter of the regime- is a city that holds dear to the traditions that survived the regime and a society reinventing itself while pushing for a better future.

CHAPTER ONE: PHNOM PENH

📷 @ALLPHOTOLONDON

Today, Phnom Penh is a city full of kindhearted people who have embraced globalization and the western world. While you can and should visit the cruel remnants of Phnom Penh's recent history such as The Killing Fields and S21 Prison, you can also embrace the new, more international side of Phnom Penh.

Rooftop pools galore, NGOs supporting the arts, fabulous western food, salsa dancing clubs, trivia nights…Phnom Penh is as modern as it gets. Consider spending a few rewarding days in this underrated city for an experience that will alter your perspective in more ways than one.

AREAS TO EXPLORE IN PHNOM PENH

Riverside

Phnom Penh's Sisowath Quay Boardwalk literally lights up at night. You can watch boats cruising along the water from your park bench. Vendors will roll by with their carts selling beers and snacks. Kids will come along to collect your cans. Locals will bring a picnic of food and a straw mat where they'll feast on local dishes. Right across the road, the main street is lined with international bars and restaurants and nearby are some of Phnom Penh's main attractions such as the Royal Palace and National Museum.

Russian Market

Also known as Toul Tom Poung in Khmer (the language of Cambodia), the Russian Market District is worth a visit. While the epicenter of this area is obviously the large market which sells fabrics and souvenirs- the area surrounding the market, offering a beautiful blend between old and new, is certainly worth a peek. Eat grilled meat from a roadside BBQ or pop into KFC to experience Cambodia's love for the colonel. Stop by a family-run shop for some instant coffee or kick your feet up at a trendy café. This is a fun area to aimlessly explore. It always ends with food.

BKK

Spas. Western food. Nightlife. Expats. Tourists. Hostels. Get the picture? Split into 3 sections: BKK1, BKK2, and BKK3 – BKK is the most modern district in Phnom Penh. You'll find all the comforts of home here but with an international twist. BKK encompasses what it's like to live abroad in Phnom Penh's melting pot district with a community of expats from around the world. With this comes Salsa nights, Trivia nights, live DJ dance parties, and an abundance of eclectic bars. Stay in this area to be close to all the action.

Prek Leap

Outside the international hustle and bustle is Prek Leap- a district where you'll find more locals, lots of Khmer food and karaoke for days! Silk Island is close by, as is the ferry terminal for any Mekong trips. You can find lots of cheap guest houses and even cheaper food around this old school district

FUN FACT!

Phnom Penh's name comes from Penh's Hill, the hill on which the Buddhist temple stands.

CHAPTER 1: **PHNOM PENH**

Where to Stay in Phnom Penh

The Bale Phnom Penh Resort
Fab-U-Lous. This resort would easily cost $700 bucks a night back in the good ol' USA. But because…Cambodia…you can stay in the lap of luxury for a fraction of the price. With only 18 rooms in the entire resort, prepare to be doted on like a queen. Spend your days at the pristine pool lined with palm trees overlooking the Mekong River, have a soak in your Jacuzzi tub, and wander the property adorned with stunning Buddha statues everywhere you look. This place is zen as fuck. Ps. For a balance of lavish life and local experience, take a day trip across the river to Koh Dach.

★ **Style:** Chic Privates
Budget: $$$$
Where: 13km North of the City Center – Riverside across from Koh Dach
Address: National Road 6A, Bridge No. 8 Sangkat Bak Khaeng

BOOK HERE

BOOKING.COM

Pavillion

For around $100 a night, you can get a gorgeous room with your very own private jacuzzi. Go skinny dipping. No tan lines here! Pool villas all booked? No worries. Every room here is glamorous and gives you access to the opulent hotel pool lined with overhanging palm trees and full bar service. This French Colonial property offers a papered oasis away from the hustle and bustle of city life. The cherry on top of your quiet ice cream Sundae? No children allowed.

★ **Style:** Privates
Budget: $$$
Where: Riverside
Address: St 19, No. 227, Daun Penh

BOOK HERE

Plantation Urban Resort & Spa

My go-to hotel whenever I visit Phnom Penh, Plantation Urban Resort offers clean & modern rooms with fabulous room service, a secure safe for your valuables, a generous buffet breakfast...and best of all, a full-service pool surrounded by lush greenery. For a moment, you forget you're even in the city. When you want to venture out, you're just a 5-minute walk to Bassac Lane (308 Street) which is a trendy little alley lined with hole-in-the-wall bars and restaurants offering fare from around the world.

★ **Style:** Privates
Budget: $$$
Where: Behind the Royal Palace
Address: # 28 Street 184, Daun Penh

BOOK HERE

Aquarius Hotel and Urban Resort

What the rooms lack in flair, the infinity pool overlooking the city certainly makes up for in brilliance. Aquarius has the best pool in the entire city with cushions for sun tanning, big umbrellas for reading, poolside service for being lazy and a see-through pool wall for America's Next Top Model – style photos. To round out the perfect hotel stay, expect gourmet food, ultra professional staff and super comfortable beds.

★ **Style:** Privates
💵 **Budget:** $$
📍 **Where:** Riverside
🏠 **Address:** #5A Street 240, Daun Penh

BOOK HERE

....

Mettavary Hotel

When you're on a tight budget but really need to get in the pool! Mettavary Hotell is a simple hotel with big rooms and a rooftop pool with lounge beds! Sometimes that is all you need. After you're done with happy hour with your toes in the water, stroll down the road to Bassac Lane (308 Street) to experience the local side of Phnom Penh. This place offers the best of both worlds without spending too much!

★ **Style:** Privates
💵 **Budget:** $$
📍 **Where:** Bassac Lane
🏠 **Address:** No.17, Street 312 corner 21

BOOK HERE

....

Mad Monkey Hostel

Mad Monkey has their shit together. Need to book a bus? Reception will do it for you. Need to extend your visa? Let them handle it. Want to go on an ATV tour through Khmer villages? Of course they do that, too. Mad Monkey makes every part of your stay so smooth- including making friends. Join the Sunset BBQ on Thursdays, Keg Parties on Sundays, Pub Crawls on Fridays and happy hour every night.

★ **Style:** Dorms & Privates
💵 **Budget:** $
📍 **Where:** BKK
🏠 **Address:** No. 3 - Off Street 310

BOOK HERE

CHAPTER 1: **PHNOM PENH**

Where to Eat in Phnom Penh

Bassac Lane
When you don't want to make formal plans, just show up to Bassac Lane. This little street will charm your pants off! You'll find hole in the wall pizza bars and white table cloth Khmer restaurants (like you'll see next). There is a social element to many of these little bars so get cute and come solo!

♥ **Where:** Put Bassac Lane into your GoogleMaps or use the next restaurant as your starting point.

ST 63 Bassac Restaurant
White table cloth venue with upscale Khmer dishes & chilled bottles of wine in a breezy outdoor setting amongst tropical plants with top-notch service…and I haven't even told you the best part yet. This place is street-food level cheap! I don't know how this family-run restaurant gets away with charging $3 for Pumpkin Curry but I'm not complaining.

☉ **Open:** Monday-Saturday 11am-11pm
🛺 **How to Get There:** Drop you off at St. 308 and go straight down the alley until you see a residential style property on your right.
🏠 **Address:** 308 St. | Just 4 doors north of 294 St.

Katy Peri's Peri Peri Chicken and Pizza
What a name. What a concept. A wood-fire pizza oven built into a Tuk Tuk that travels around Phnom Penh serving pizza to the masses. Pizza so good that this oven on wheels is legendary in Phnom Penh and has amassed a loyal following. Starting at $2.50 for a Margherita pizza, it's easy to fall in love and lust with these sexy pies.

Open: 9:30 - Late
How to Get There: Take a Pass App!
Address: Daily on Street 51, Corner 172 / Monday + Thursday at Showbox Bar

The Sushi Bar (1 BKK)

Sushi? In Phnom Penh? I used to be skeptical, too but I love this place. Every time I go in, it's filled with Japanese patrons sipping on Miso Soup and scarfing down large sushi platters with nigiri and generous rolls. Prices are cheap and portions are enough to fill you up. While the sushi isn't out of this world amazing- it certainly hits the spot. Also, expect a 10% service charge. It's stupid but if you know beforehand, you're less likely to be annoyed when you get your bill.

Open: Everyday 11am-10pm
Where: BKK 1 – up the road from Mad Monkey
Address: 2D, Street 302 (Use Mad Monkey as your starting point)

David's Noodle Restaurant

You've never had noodles this fresh! They are literally made right in front of your eyes! Enjoy artisan dumplings and noodles from scratch when you dine at David's Restaurant in Phnom Penh. The dumpling soup is one of the most popular and most recommended dishes here! One bite and you'll understand why locals and visitors alike end up eating here 3-4 times per week.

Open: Everyday 10am-10pm
Where: Near the Royal Palace
Address: No. 213, 13 Preah Ang Eng St. (13)

Daughters of Cambodia

In Cambodia, the sex trade is still a harsh reality. Escaping the sex trade is only step 1 to rehabilitation. Step 2 is creating a new life for yourself. Daughters of Cambodia Visitor Centre is a community based restaurant where former victims of sex trafficking are given a chance to start over by acquiring culinary skills and training in hospitality.

Feel good in your heart and in your tummy by eating some delicious culinary creations. Have a fresh salad, some crisp fish and chips, and take some pastries to go. The food is definitely on point here.

⊙ **Open:** Monday-Saturday 9am – 5:30pm
📍 **Where:** The Riverside
🏠 **Address:** 321 Sisowath Quay

Next, hit up the markets. Around every market in Southeast Asia, you will find a rich street food culture. See the stalls with lots of people? That's where you want to eat.

📷 PISETHNIKA

FUN FACT!
Cambodia is one of the only few countries in the world that has never ever had a McDonalds.

CHAPTER 1: **PHNOM PENH**

Sights & History in Phnom Penh

To see these sights, hire a Tuk Tuk for the day and make it a tour - but hire one off the street. They'll charge you ⅓ of the price of the tours you'll find online.

The Killing Fields
The Killing Fields are emotional and for some, down right gut wrenching- but if you want to grasp the reality of what happened here in Cambodia, you need to see this with your own eyes.

This particular killing field in Phnom Penh is where hundreds of thousands of men, women, and children were brought and killed during the Khmer Rouge. Their bodies were stacked in huge ditches in the ground where their bones still remain. The large pits where human bones and clothing stick out from the ground have not been staged for dramatics. In fact, when heavy rains fall on these fields, more and more undiscovered bones tend to rise up out of the earth.

Upon your visit to the field, you'll be given a headset that will guide you through, painting the picture of the monstrous acts that happened here with narration and personal stories from survivors. Walk silently and respectfully as you take it all in.

The Tuol Sleng Genocide Museum - S21 Prison
When the Khmer Rouge took power in Phnom Penh, they needed a place to gather, brutalize, and interrogate their victims. So, they converted a local high school into a torture prison. Over 4 years, 14,000 people entered this prison and only 7 survived.

Today, the prison has been turned into a museum with photos of prisoners on the walls, torture chambers still in place, and firsthand stories from family members of the victims who lost their lives here. In some areas of the prison, there are scratch marks on the walls and blood stained into the floor. This is truly a step back in time, allowing you to fully comprehend how these victims suffered.

Many people join their visits to The Killing Fields and the S21 prison into one somber day with a tuk tuk driver and then go for much-needed beers afterwards to process what they've just experienced.

RANT FROM ALEXA...
I once heard a snippity "travel expert" say that visiting the Killing Fields is part of "dark tourism" or a morbid fascination with other countries - and I couldn't disagree more. This is history. If we don't learn from history, what are we even doing here? If we aren't trying to understand a culture or society and its current state of being, why are we even traveling? You go here because you're an explorer and not a tourist. And I like the way you travel.

The Silver Pagoda
This gorgeous Buddhist temple represents the epitome of South East Asian culture. From the shiny golden roof to the monks dressed in bright orange, the Silver Pagoda brings everything you envisioned about Cambodia to life.

As you approach the entrance of the temple, you'll realize why this temple is called the "Silver Pagoda". The floor is covered in 5,000 glittering silver tiles as a gift to Buddha. To protect these tiles, you cannot walk on them but you can look.

Head up the grand staircase and you'll be led to the Temple of the Emerald Buddha, sparkling in 2086 diamonds! As if that wasn't lavish enough, this Buddha sits next to an 80kg bronze Buddha, a pure gold Buddha AND a silver-gold Buddha, each with its own story to tell.

Wat Phnom

You won't find many hills in Phnom Penh, and certainly not many covered in grass and trees. That's what makes Wat Phnom so special. Sitting atop a 27 meter-high grassy knoll with scattered trees is Wat Phnom, a pagoda that is said to have first been built in the 1300's. Climb the wide staircase lined with Buddha statues and lions and you'll be met with a traditional temple holding an extraordinary purpose.

Home to 4 statues of Buddha, Wat Phnom now serves as a place for local school kids to pray to Buddha for good marks on their school exams and for gamblers to pray for good luck in the casino. Try it out for yourself- it couldn't hurt!

You can easily visit these next places on your own…

FUN FACT!

Becasue of its French architecture around the city, Phnom Penh has been often called "The Paris of the East".

Visit the National Museum

With ancient artifacts from the 1600s, cultural performances by Khmer dancers, tributes to Cambodian warriors, replicas of traditional Khmer houses, and a peek into modern day farming life - the National Museum is a comprehensive representation of Khmer culture, old and new - all housed in gorgeous 1920's inspired temple architecture with golden tiled roofs that glitter in the sun.

Budget: $5-$10, depending on whether you opt for the audio guide to take you through the museum.
Open: Everyday 8am – 5pm
Where: Riverside
Address: Preah Ang Eng St. (13)

The Royal Palace

Built in the 1860's, this opulent palace has since served as the royal residence in Phnom Penh, discounting a brief point of abandonment during the Khmer Rouge.

The entire complex sits riverside where you can watch motorboats floating on by and capture some great photos of daily river life in Phnom Penh. You'll get a chance to learn about the history of the royal family in Cambodia and the history of this complex city.

When you visit, dress appropriately for Buddhist culture. Women should cover their knees and shoulders while men should wear shirts with sleeves.

Budget: $6.50 solo - $10 with a guide
Open: Everyday 8am – 10:30am / 2pm – 5pm
Where: Riverside
Address: Samdach Sothearos Blvd (3)

CHAPTER 1: **PHNOM PENH**

Fun Things in Phnom Penh

Have a Pool Day
I swear, there are more hotels with rooftop pools than not. However, if you aren't staying at a rooftop pool hotel, I've got one for you. Aquarius Hotel has an amazing infinity pool overlooking the riverside AND has one of those clear pool walls- amazing for taking underwater photos. Outside guests are welcome to come use the pool and lounge under big umbrellas as long as you order a drink or food (both of which are awesome here).

Open: 9am-9pm
Budget: Price of drink or food
Where: Aquarius Hotel
Address: No 5, St 240, Sangkat Chakto Mukh

Go Salsa Dancing
With its vibrant international community, Phnom Penh is a fabulous city for salsa dancing with partners from all over the world. Check out the Facebook Group below for the schedule! No partner required- this is a great way for solo girl travelers to meet other people!

Budget: Some classes are free!
Where: BKK1
Address: Duplex Belgian Tavern #3 St 278 Sangkat BKK1
Facebook Group: Salsa Phnom Penh

Bear Care Tour
Sun Bears and Moon Bears are indigenous to Asia, but their habitats are slowly being destroyed. Free the Bears is a sanctuary that focuses on bear habitat conservation and species preservation. That means baby bears!

When you visit the center, you can see the happy bears playing in their enclosed forest habitats, and learn what the bears eat. You'll make snacks for the bears and then hide the snacks within their enclosure for them to forage and find later.

Budget: $90 per person
Where: 8am pick up from Joma Cafe, corner of Norodom and Street 294
Open: All day from 8am-5:30pm
Visit them at www.freethebears.org

Take a (Classy) Booze Cruise on the Mekong

In Phnom Penh, you'll find lots of companies that offer Sunset Cocktail River Cruises with cocktails, beer and wine. Sip slowly as you pass the Royal Palace and watch the sun go down over the river. This cruise lasts about 1 ½ hours and is a perfect way to see the city.

Budget: $
Where: Hotel pick up   **Book here:**

Visit Koh Dach (Silk Island)

Take a peek into rural Cambodia – just a few miles away from the city center. Situated just north of Phnom Penh, you can hop on a quick ferry alongside traveling chickens, jackfruit and families who will stare at you like you're Big Foot. The Silk Village is full of traditional Khmer houses on stilts- all of which have a silk weaving machine below, as silk weaving is the island's specialty. The people here are poor but the hospitality is overwhelming. Hire a Tuk Tuk to take you around for the day, join a tour, or go on your own to explore. Visit the silk worm farm where most of Phnom Penh's silk is produced and buy a few scarves directly from the source.

Budget: Ferry tickets are $1
Where: North of Phnom Penh
How to Get There: Take a Tuk Tuk to the pier

CHAPTER 1: **PHNOM PENH**

Shopping (and more eating) in Phnom Penh

The Old Market
Rise and shine, kiddos! Vendors are up at 5am waiting to sell you some delicious fruit! The Old Market, also known as Phsar Chas, is an authentic Cambodian market known to the locals as the best spot for produce shopping. If you want to taste truly fresh and organic mangos or jackfruit- this is the place!

Located in the Old French Quarter next to the river, this market is the perfect place to start your morning. Sit on a bench with your fresh finds and watch morning traffic zooming with motorbikes and food vendors feeding workers galore on their way to work.

The Russian Market
Many tuk tuk drivers will call out to you on the streets offering to take you to the Russian Market. It's called "The Russian Market" as this was the most popular area amongst Russian expats back in the 1980s. You'll find a few "Russian" things here like Russian dolls and small Russian flags, but the bulk of the selection is classically Cambodian. You can expect to find great souvenirs like silk scarves, spices, wood carvings, and more.

As one of the largest markets with the widest variety of goods in Phnom Penh, the Russian Market is the best market to visit if you're short on time as you'll find a little bit of everything here.

PRO TIP: Bring a bottle of water with you or buy one as soon as you get there - this market tends to tire you out with the heat.

Central Market
This huge golden dome market in the center of Phnom Penh has literally every item you could ever want to buy while on vacation. Need sunglasses? They have hundreds. In the market for a knock-off NBA cap? They're reppin' every team. Looking for children's clothes to send back to your niece and nephew? Outfit them like an adorable Khmer kid. You could easily spend hours wandering this market!

When you get hungry, they've got row after row of Khmer food stands selling fried fish, hot soup, and an array of fried bugs and spiders! Bring your camera as there are plenty of novel things to see here.

The Olympic Market
If you were thinking of having a dress or custom bed sheets made, then pick out some fantastic fabrics at the Olympic Market. With three levels and hundreds of fabric stalls, take your time feeling your way through. You can haggle with vendors and also ask them for advice in choosing the right fabric for your intended design.

You'll come across a few tailors in the plaza who can create what it is that you've dreamed up. If you can't spot a tailor on your own, ask the fabric vendors where to find one and they'll point you in the right direction!

Phnom Penh Night Market
After a rough day of cultural sightseeing, treat yourself to the modern pleasures of Cambodian life at the Phnom Penh Night Market. Interact with cheerful vendors selling clothing, jewelry, bags, shoes, dishes, hardware, and a collection of small trinkets that make for perfect souvenirs

Just like any fabulous night market, you'll find lots of Cambodian food here, too. Grilled meat on sticks, noodle soups, dried seafood, fruit shakes and more. Nearby are plastic tables and chairs where you can gather all your goodies and have a feast.

CHAPTER 1: **PHNOM PENH**

Spas & Salons in Phnom Penh

Bliss Spa Cambodia
Take advantage of these prices! Go all out with a lavish 2-hour experience including a body scrub with Himalayan salts, an aroma massage, and a scalp massage. For the "Royal Indulgence", spend 3 hours with an herbal steam treatment, a body scrub, a Balinese massage, and a rejuvenation facial. There are Khmer Massages, detox treatments, and even massages for babies. This place does it all for great prices, in a truly serene environment and by professional relaxation specialists.

🕑 **Open:** Everyday 9am-9pm
📍 **Where:** Near Independence Monument
🏠 **Address:** Oknha Chhun St. (240)

The Doll House Cambodia
Balayage. Hair extensions. Layers. Foils. The stylists at The Doll House in Phnom Penh will fix those travel tresses with care. And if you need to nourish your dried out locks before you fly home, try a Keratin Treatment at a fraction of the price that you'd pay in the west!

🕑 **Open:** Tuesday-Saturday 9am-7pm / Sunday 11am -7pm
📍 **Where:** Bassac Lane
🏠 **Address:** No M114 Bassac Lane - Off Street 308

"A nomad I will remain for life,
in love with distant and uncharted places."

- **ISABELLE EBERHARDT**

CHAPTER 1: **PHNOM PENH**

Nightlife in Phnom Penh

You can enter all of these destinations into GoogleMaps or your RideShare App

Pub Street
As with any pub street around the world, weekends tend to be more crazy than weekdays. On Pub Street, you get a collection of local expats and travelers who crowd into popular bars like Top Banana where draft beer is $1 and appetizers are $3. This small stretch of street is enough to keep any traveler entertained for a long evening out.
Google Maps: Top Banana

Bassac Lane (Street 308)
Bassac Lane is a picturesque little street lined with upscale bars, dive restaurants, and gourmet eateries. Jetting off from Bassac Lane, you'll find a winding little alley with a collection of hole-in-the-wall bars that cater to both a Khmer and Western clientele. Hop from one spot to another on foot until the night is through.

Street 51
Heart of Darkness, Shanghai, White Cobra, Black Cat…with names like these, you can probably guess that these bars aren't playing around. They take cocktails and atmosphere to the next level with quirky décor and gorgeous drinks. Once your buzz kicks in, wander Street 51 where you'll find night clubs, Billiard bars, and the widely popular Walkabout Hotel Bar and Restaurant which is open 24/7. This is a fun street for people watching, partying, and drunk eating.

CHAPTER 1: **PHNOM PENH**

How to Get Around in Phnom Penh

PassApp
Phnom Penh's version of Uber, PassApp is a transportation app that saves you the headache of giving directions to and haggling with a Tuk Tuk driver. It's the safest, most reliable way to travel around Phnom Penh as a visitor. And instead of a car, you'll be picked up in a cute little Indian-style rickshaw! Just type in your destination, the app detects your location. No getting lost or turned around. Pay in cash. Most trips are less than $1 on PassApp. ***Pro Tip:*** *You'll need an international phone number or a Cambodian Sim card to work with this app. Make sure you pick one up ASAP.*

Tuk Tuks
Tuk Tuk drivers are everywhere! Flag one down and for $2-$5, they'll take you where you need to go. Find one that speaks a decent amount of English? Take his number down for future trips! You can also hire a Tuk Tuk driver for an entire day or half day to take you sightseeing around the city (for usually $20). ***Pro Tip:*** *Keep your bags and phones close or concealed in the tuk tuk- otherwise it might get snatched in traffic.*

Walking
During the day, you're safe to walk around the markets, along the riverside, and down the main roads of BKK. At night, however, refrain from walking at all costs (other than the riverside area). Take a Tuk Tuk or a PassApp.

Private Taxi
Long distance or full-day tours can be way more comfortable in a comfy, air conditioned car rather than a bumpy bus. Most taxis here are private (entrepreneur drivers) and are in the form of Lexus SUVs. Khmers love them.

CHAPTER 1: **PHNOM PENH**

Crime & Safety in Phnom Penh

Petty Theft is Widespread
Stealing phones and purses- that is the specialty of thieves in Phnom Penh. But don't let this whole theft thing freak you out BECAUSE thieves look for travelers who have their guard down. They look for the easiest targets possible because even thieves are lazy. You're already reading this which means that you've lowered the chances that you'll become a victim.

Watch out for these Thievery Tactics:

▲ Tactic: Motorbikes following you at night
❷ What to Do: Make eye contact, give them a bitch face and tell them to go away. Talk to them, let them know that you see them. Many times the thieves are kids. Confrontation is enough to fend them off.

▲ Tactic: Swooping a phone out of a texter's hands
❷ What to Do: Text on your phone like your sexting at the dinner table. Hide it so that it is difficult to see.

▲ Tactic: Reaching inside of the Tuk Tuk and driving off with your bag.
❷ What to Do: Keep your purse behind your body in the Tuk Tuk and physically clip your larger bags to the Tuk Tuk.

"We travel, some of us forever, to seek other states, other lives, other souls."

— ANAÏS NIN

CHAPTER 1: PHNOM PENH

How to Get to Phnom Penh

FROM SIEM REAP

By Plane
- **Point of Departure:** Siem Reap Airport
- **When:** All day every day
- **Duration:** 45 Minutes
- **Budget:** $70+

By Bus
For the safest, most comfortable journey, always go with Giant Ibis Bus company.
- **Point of Departure:** Giant Ibis Bus Terminal
- **When:** Daily 8:45 am, 9 am, 9:45 am, 12:30 pm, 10:30 pm, 11 pm, 11:30 pm.
- **Duration:** 7 Hours
- **Budget:** $15
- **Book:** www.12go.asia/en

PRO TIP
Take one of the night buses to get a cozy sleep and save money on accommodation!

By Private Taxi
- **Point of Departure:** Pick up at your hotel
- **When:** Whenever you want
- **Duration:** 4-5 hours
- **Budget:** $70-90
- **Book:** Facebook Group 'Taxi Share Cambodia'

By Boat
Point of Departure: Minivan pick up from your hotel
When: During the months of July and March (when water levels are ideal) – everyday at 7am
Duration: 4 – 6 Hours
Budget: $18-$35 depending on the boat company

PRO TIPS
- Only take the boat when the weather is bright and sunny!
- Buying tickets through a travel agency or your hotel is cheaper than buying at the dock.
- Bring snacks. Hell, bring meals.
- Avoid a company called Mekong Cruise

FROM BATTAMBANG

By MiniBus
Point of Departure: Battambang Bus Terminal
When: Daily 7:30 am, 8:30 am, 2:30 pm, 5:30 pm
Duration: 5.5 Hours
Budget: $14
Book: www.12go.asia/en

By Private Taxi
Point of Departure: Pick up at your hotel
When: Whenever you want
Duration: 4-5 hours
Budget: $60-80
Book: Facebook Group 'Taxi Share Cambodia'

FROM SIHANOUKVILLE

Ø By Plane
Point of Departure: Sihanoukville Airport
When: 6 Flights per day – 7:05 am, 1:55 pm, 2:45 pm, 4:25 pm, 5:30 pm, 6:10pm

Duration: 35 Minutes
Budget: $80-100

PRO TIP
Planes are small and bumpy! Expect these flights to have luggage fees, as well.

By Taxi
Point of Departure: Pick up at your hotel
When: Whenever you want
Duration: 4.5 hours
Budget: $45-60
Book: See our section titled 'Driver Directory'

By Minivan
Point of Departure: Pick up at your hotel
When: All day every day
Duration: 5-6 hours
Budget: $10-12
Book: With your hotel/hostel/guesthouse

FROM THAILAND

By Bus
There will be bathroom breaks, snack breaks, and lots of time to sleep.
Point of Departure: Bangkok - Mo Chit Bus Terminal (Northern Bus Terminal)
When: Every day at 5am
Duration: 13 Hours
Budget: $15-30 USD

PRO TIP
Book with a company called 'Giant Ibis' for the most comfortable and reliable journey. This bus journey is pretty comfortable considering its long duration, the staff are professional, AND they hand out snacks and water during the trip.

When you get to the border, you can leave your bags on the bus. You'll cross immigration and the bus will meet you on the other side. Check out our Visa and Immigration section on page 10 for more info on how this process works!

By Plane
- **Point of Departure:** Bangkok Airports
- **When:** All day every day
- **Duration:** 1 Hour
- **Budget:** $60-100

PRO TIP
There are 2 airports in Bangkok! Check your ticket twice!

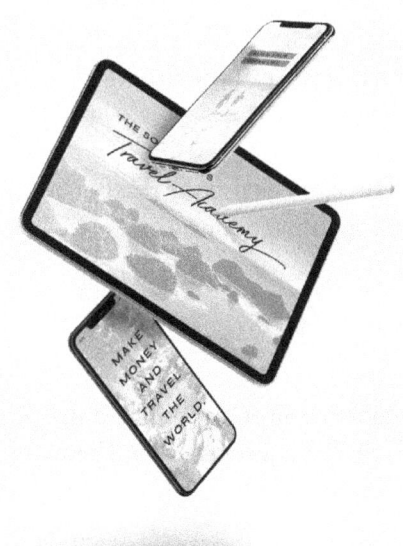

THE SOLO GIRL'S

Travel Academy

Have you ever wanted to just pack it all up and go?

Travel the world solo, escape the monotony of the 9–5, and trade the politics for purpose.

That's what I did.

And now, I'm teaching you how to do the same.

 Join me at SoloGirlsTravelAcademy.

CHAPTER 1: **PHNOM PENH**

From the Phnom Penh Airport into Town

For an international airport, Phnom Penh Airport is quite small and easy to navigate. There's one arrival hall, one immigration checkpoint and one main exit. Easy peasy.

Okay- let's get you into town…

○ Option 1: Hire a Car to Pick you Up

My favorite option! Have a car waiting for you at the airport with your cute lil' name on a sign.

An easy way to do get a trustworthy driver is here on GetYourGuide ☞

📍**Where:** They'll be waiting for you right when you exit the airport.
💸**Budget:** $20-$30 or less

Message one of my drivers in my Drivery Directory or visit the Facebook Page 'Taxi Share Cambodia' to wrangle an English-speaking driver in no time.

○ Option 2: Uber or Grab Taxi

All you need to do is buy a SIM card outside the airport ($5), fire it up and order your car. Uber is…Uber. And Grab Taxi is just like Uber. These apps will be life savers during your trip in Phnom Penh.

Where: At the arrivals gate, right when you exit the airport.
How Much: Typically $15 or less

○ Option 3: Jump in a Tuk Tuk

Start your trip off with some excitement as your Tuk Tuk weaves around traffic and bounces over potholes. This is a fun option for someone who is traveling with a backpack that is easy to hold along the way.

♀ Where: Walk through the parking lot and exit the airport. There will be Tuk Tuks lined around the perimeter, having just dropped off other guests.
🏷 Budget: $5-$8

AIRPORT PRO TIPS

✈ I wouldn't recommend hiring a Taxi or Tuk Tuk from the tourist stands inside the airport- their prices tend to be higher.

✈ There will be taxi drivers that approach you the second you step outside of the airport. They'll be offering you rides. Rides that start at pretty expensive prices. If you can haggle them down to the prices that you've read about here today, there's no harm in driving with these guys.

✈ A public bus does exist but girl, it's slow and old and just not worth it.

TRAVEL NOTES:

....

....

....

....

CHAPTER TWO

Siem Reap

📷 @SOUVENIRPIXELS

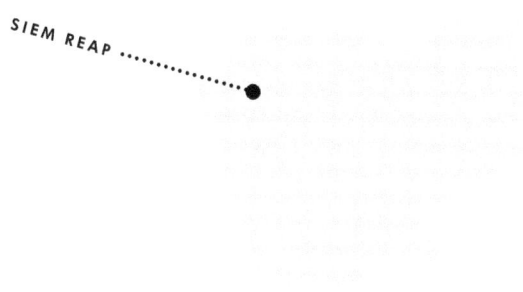

CHAPTER TWO

Siem Reap

Outside of the mystifying temple tours of Angkor Wat, this northern city has a lot to offer in terms of culture, history, and wild holiday antics. Dive into cooking classes and pottery-making lessons, visit war museums to learn about the areas affected by landmines, and then mingle with other travelers at some local pubs where you can find amazing Western food and low-priced draft beer.

Siem Reap offers extremely comfortable accommodation options spanning from budget hostels to luxurious hotels with pristine pools. It is easy to spend a week or so just exploring all of the prized features that Siem Reap has to offer.

AREAS TO EXPLORE IN SIEM REAP

Old Market
Old Market refers to both the actual market (Psar Chaa) and the busy area that surrounds it. Most people stay in the Old Market area when they visit Siem Reap because it's convenient and where all the action is. This area is full of hotels, within walking distance to a variety of markets and has all of the western amenities that you need!

Pub Street

This long walking road is lined with neon signs, bars touting bucket drink specials, a small market, and groups of social travelers everywhere you turn. You'll find plenty of clubs and watering holes that are open late, as well as, lots of budget hostels in the area making for a convenient place to crash. Pub Street has become the official backpacker's oasis, and it's easy to see why.

Alley West

Just to the west of the Old Market is this artsy little street lined with cute cafes and charitable handicraft stores. This area is more modern with refurbished buildings and European accents. It's a great place for shopping and eating…but also for some stunning photography.

Wat Bo Road and Surrounding Area

Just across the river is Wat Bo Road – an area with trendy restaurants, classy bars, yummy cafes, upscale Khmer food, and local shops. Tucked away from the party vibes of Pub Street, sleeping on this side of the river ensures a bit more peace and quiet. You'll find nice hotels over water catering to an older crowd.

HUMPHREY MULEBA

CHAPTER 2: **SIEM REAP**

Where to Stay in Siem Reap

FCC Angkor

Treat yo self, girl. FCC is one classy joint. You'll be treated like royalty the moment you check in. Take a dip in the glamorous pool and have a soak in the spacious bath tub. Enjoy room service eaten on your private terrace or hit the restaurant for some of the best eats in Siem Reap. And while this place may be fancy, beer on tap is still around $2 per pint. Heads up, this place is a 15-minute walk to the market or Pub Street, BUT they've got a Tuk Tuk on staff to drop you off wherever you need to go.

★ **Style:** Privates
Budget: $$$
Where: Next to the River & Royal Gardens – 7 minute Tuk Tuk to Pub Street
Address: Pokambor Ave

BOOK HERE

....

Golden Temple Hotel

5-star service with 3-star prices. You'll be blown away by the royal treatment and amenities at Golden Temple Hotel. With stunning architecture and glamorous decor, prepare for a photoshoot. But truly, it's the staff that make this place memorable. If it's in your budget, don't hesitate to spoil yourself here. Bonus: You're just a 7-minute walk from Pub Street.

★ **Style:** Privates
Budget: $$$
Where: 7 minute walk to Pub Street
Address: Angkor High School Road

BOOK HERE

Bayon Boutique Hotel

When you're in a social mood...but not a party mood, Bayon Boutique Hotel is the best place to meet other travelers with whom you can enjoy yummy food and good conversation by the pool. Venture out with your new pals to explore the area. This is a prime location! And there's nothing like coming back to a quiet dorm with crisp clean sheets after a hot day of sightseeing.

★ **Style:** Privates
💰 **Budget:** $$
📍 **Where:** Next to Khmer Pub Lane
🏨 **Address:** Steung Siem Reap, Svay Dangkum

BOOK HERE

Onederz Hostel

Pool party time! Everyone at Onederz Hostel is there for the same 2 reasons: to visit Angkor Wat and to socialize with people from around the world. If you're traveling solo, don't hesitate to throw yourself in the mix. The hostel is brand new with 1 ground level pool and 1 rooftop pool with sunset views. The beds are comfy, lockers are secure, and staff are super helpful when you need to book a tour or transportation.

★ **Style:** Dorms & Privates
💰 **Budget:** $
📍 **Where:** Right next to Angkor Night Market
🏨 **Address:** Corner of Taphul Road & Angkor Night Market Street

BOOK HERE

FUN FACT!

Cambodia's name has changed 5 times over the years, with every new government. It finally came back to its original name "Kingdom of Cambodia" in 1993.

Cambana d'Angkor Suites

After a day of sightseeing in the heat, come back to your own personal oasis at this intimate boutique hotel. A wonderland of elephant carvings, vibrant historical paintings and tall green jungle foliage really makes you feel like you're in Cambodia, while the modern amenities immediately transfer you into vacation mode. Swim in the pool, have a cappuccino in the café and enjoy the smiles and care of the super attentive, English-speaking Khmer staff.

★ **Style:** Privates
Budget: $$
Where: Next to Khmer Pub Lane
Address: Road No. 6, Salakanseng Village, Svay Dangkum Commune

BOOK HERE

BOOKING.COM

CHAPTER 2: **SIEM REAP**

Where to Eat in Siem Reap

Fresh Fruit Factory
Make a breakfast reservation (a few days in advance) to take a bite out of this colorful café. Passion Fruit Pancakes, Mango French Toast, Smoothie Bowls and the famous Ice Mountain topped with whichever fresh fruit speaks to your taste buds. Here, you can eat super clean! Clean, fresh fruit from Cambodia, clean kitchen, and clean water give you peace of mind for your tummy's first few days abroad.

⊙ **Open:** Tuesday-Sunday 11am – 8pm
♀ **Where:** Next to the Angkor National Museum
🏠 **Address:** #155 Taphul Road
f **Reservations on Facebook:** Fresh Fruit Factory

The Missing Socks Laundry Café
I love this place for breakfast, brunch & lunch. It's all about the waffles. Order classic waffles with bacon and eggs or step outside the bun with a waffle burger. Every plate is perfection. Don't worry if you slop on yourself, this place is also a laundromat. Get your clothes cleaned while you sip on artisan coffee. You'll leave a clean and caffeinated woman!

⊙ **Open:** Daily 7am-7pm
♀ **Where:** East of Pub Street by S Hotel and Kochi-ke hostel.
🏠 **Address:** #55 Steung Thmey Village

Mahob Khmer Cuisine

Cambodian Food at its finest! Here, the Khmer chef and restaurateur utilizes quintessential Asian ingredients to elevate classic Khmer dishes to modern works of culinary art. Local clams with tamarind sauce, slow braised oxtail, deep fried frog legs- you'll never truly understand Khmer cuisine until you dine at Mahob. The entire experience is set in a traditional wooden Khmer house on stilts with lush greenery all around you. So sublime.

Open: Daily 11:30am -10:30pm
Where: North of the Night Market
Address: River Rd, Krong

Street Food

South East Asia is all about street food! Where vendors load their ingredients into carts to feed the working class, this is one of the most authentic ways to experience local cuisine. Visit the Old Market for some spring rolls or try some ice cream made on the spot with cold-plate food carts outside of Pub Street.

PRO TIP ABOUT STREET FOOD:
Street Food in Cambodia can be sketchier than in Vietnam or Malaysia. Outside of the two street food areas above, eat with caution. If you want to go on a super yummy street food tour with vendors that have been vetted for clean eats, go on the Street Food Tour with a company called **River Garden's Tour** for $25 per person.

CHAPTER 2: **SIEM REAP**

Sights & History in Siem Reap

Angkor Wat Temple

📷 @ALLPHOTOLONDON

This is a bucket list experience! To explore the 500 acre kingdom of Angkor Wat, the largest Buddhist temple on earth which also serves as the capital of the Khmer Empire from the 9th to the 15th century which took 30 years to build.

The temples are unbelievably complex. Crumblings slowly as the jungle takes them over, you can explore each complex while ducking under stone archways or following vine covered stairways. It feels as if you've been transported back in time into a world long forgotten.

…until you see the tourists. Yes, many many tourists come to Angkor Wat, specifically at sunrise. To avoid the tourists, avoid the sunrise tour. It's pretty but it's not worth it sitting amongst hundreds of people with their phone out. And then, immediately following sunrise, that entire herd of humans is released into the temple.

◷ **Best times to come:** 2pm-6pm.

To explore Angkor Wat, you can come to see the main temples for just one day. Or you can dive deep to explore temples off the beaten path over 3-5 days.

◷ **Open:** Daily, 5am - 6pm
📍 **Where:** Angkor Archaeological Park
💸 **Budget:** One day $37, three days $62, five days $72.

FUN FACT: Over 2 million tourists visit Angkor Wat each year.

THE BEST WAYS TO TOUR THE TEMPLES
You need a guide. Without someone to tell you what you're seeing, you'll miss the magic of Angkor Wat.

The best place to look for tours is on GetYourGuide here ☞

But here are some tours I recommend.

 01 Siem Reap: Angkor Wat: Small-Group Sunrise Tour
An early tour with a small group and tour guides that have fun. They'll even take photos of you along the way!

02 Angkor Wat: Vintage Jeep with Driver Rental
Don't want to walk your butt around in the heat? Get a private pick up from your hotel and spend the day off roading in a jeep with the wind in your hair. You'll hop out with your guide to learn about the temples and then off to the next sights you go.

03 Bicycle tours with GrasshopperAdventures.com
Get those endorphins pumping with a 25-30km bicycle tour through the ancient kingdom of Angkor Wat. Grasshopper Adventures offers a unique way to soak up all the history and culture that this temple city has to offer at a much more efficient and enjoyable pace than walking.

You'll travel down red dirt roads through the jungle to visit Angkor Thom, Banyon, Tha Prom, and then the Elephant Terrace where you'll have lunch. Your bicycle guide will be able to fill you in on all of the interesting facts and info to complete the experience.

The tour starts at 7:30am when the weather is perfectly pleasant and goes until 4:30pm.

04 DIY Exploring on a Budget

Hire a Tuk Tuk!

Just hire a guy on the road, preferably one that speaks decent English, to take you to Angkor Wat. With your private guide, you can pick and choose the temples you want to see and decide the length of your excursion.

I usually find a tuk tuk driver I like the day before I want to go, then arrange my pick-up for the next morning. If you want to go for sunrise, arrange your pick up at 4:30am. You'll walk through the dark and wait along the edge of the ancient library pools with Angkor Wat in the background until the sun begins to rise. Have your camera ready; the sight is incredible. Getting to the temples early helps you avoid the midday heat and large tour groups.

Before you enter the complex, download the app called Angkor Wat SmartGuide. This app uses GPS to track when you've arrived at a point of interest within the temple complex and then shares with you all the fun facts and history you need to know.

PRO TIP! Ask your tuk tuk driver to take you to his village for lunch or dinner.

ANGKOR WAT FUN FACTS...

Angkor Wat in is the largest religious monument in the world.

It is estimated that 750,000 Khmer people lived in Angkor during its glory.

The compound of this temple city is bigger than Paris.

ANGKOR WAT TEMPLES TO KNOW

Angkor Wat
Although we often refer to the entire City of Temples as "Angkor Wat", Angkor War only refers to one complex of temples in the collection. Angkor Wat is the most well-known temple as it has become the country's national symbol, even being printed on the national flag.

Angkor Wat represents classic Khmer architecture and has been impressively preserved. With a beautiful pond at its feet, Angkor Wat offers the most gorgeous sites of sunrise you've ever seen.

Bayon
The official temple of Mahayana Buddhist King Jayavarman VII, Bayon is the quintessential visualization and representation of Angkorian art. The massive carving clusters replicate large royal heads complete with jewelry and extremely detailed faces. This is what you came here to see!

Behind this amazing baroque masterpiece are mythological tales and historical ties to ancient civilizations that represent a multitude of religious beliefs and centuries of royal rule.

@TAYLOR.G.SIMPSON

Ta Prohm

It's the Indiana Jones-esque lost-city vibes that make Ta Prohm a must-see temple in Angkor Wat. Built as a Mahayana Buddhist monastery and university where nearly 2,500 monks once roamed, this temple has remained relatively intact with a dusting of dilapidation giving it a mysteriously eerie atmosphere that is absolutely surreal. The stand out feature of this ancient structure is the massive tree trunk that has grown right up the center of the temple, looking as if a giant hand has a hold of the ruins.

Banteay Srei

This red sandstone shrine is quite unique in comparison to the prevailing dark gray temples both for its bright color and its miniature stature. With ornate carvings of beautiful Khmer women, Banteay Srei is regarded as a true piece of art. Created to show respect towards the Hindu god Shiva, this monument has found lots of opposition in this Buddhist culture and has faced defacing and vandalism. For this reason, extra restoration and conservation efforts have been dedicated to Banteay Srei.

Preah Khan

The temple with the most opulent history has got to be Preah Khan, the previous center of the royal dynasties of Yasovarman II and Tribhuvanadityavarman. Home to multiple shrines, there were once 430 religious deities represented at Preah Khan, which made this both a royal and holy site. During the height of Angkorian times, 10,000 servants used to walk these hallways while the royal family was dripping in gold, jewels, and fragrances. This royal existence can be seen in the detailed carvings all along the walls, creating a historic gallery and museum.

MORE ANGKOR WAT FUN FACTS...

During the 1970s, hundreds of Cambodian citizens took refuge in Angkor Wat during the civil war.

50% of Cambodia's tourism industry is generated by tourists who've come to see the Angkor Wat.

These monuments contain more sandstone than the Egyptian pyramids.

DO'S AND DON'TS OF ANGKOR WAT

Do's

♥ **Do Dress Appropriately:** Angkor Wat is a religious site so cover your shoulders and knees if you want to be respectful.

♥ **Do Explore Respectfully:** Believe it or not, in just the past few years, tourists have been punished for smashing ancient statues, writing on temple walls, and even having nude photo shoots. Come on, people!

♥ **Do Wear Comfortable Shoes:** There is lots of walking to be done! Uneven terrain is not conducive with wedge shoes or stiff sandals. Sneakers or tennis shoes are ideal for climbing stairs and wandering for hours at a time, however, comfortable sandals or flip-flops will do the trick.

Don'ts

✘ **Don't Take Souvenirs:** You'd think this would be common sense, but apparently it isn't. Not only is it illegal to steal artifacts from Angkor Wat, but it is also extremely disrespectful to the spirits that locals believe still reside in this city.

✘ **Don't Explore Hung-over:** This is a once in a lifetime experience! Plan accordingly. Get some good sleep the night before so that you can absorb all the history and handle all the walking.

What to Bring to the Temples:
→ Sunglasses
→ Sunscreen
→ Fully charged camera
→ 1.5 liter of water per person
→ Snacks (peanuts, almonds, fruit)
→ A day bag for all of the above
→ Super comfy walking shoes or sandals
→ A scarf or sweater to cover your shoulders

PRO TIP BEFORE YOU GO

Do some stretches, drink plenty of water, and try not to be hungover- you're in for a long yet extremely fulfilling day that you will genuinely never forget.

CHAPTER 2: SIEM REAP

Fun Things to do in Siem Reap

Phare: The Cambodian Circus
A mesmerizing circus with a humanitarian cause, Phare puts on a thrilling show with fire, acrobatics, and entrancing music that is worth every penny. The passionate performers are former street kids or low-income artists who receive free circus and art education by Phare. Memorable, inspirational, and charitable, this one is a MUST when visiting Siem Reap!

🎟️ **Budget:** $38 USD
🕖 **Open:** Daily at 7pm
📍 **Where:** Phare Circus Ring Road, south of the intersection with Sok San Road
🌐 Visit pharecircus.org for tickets

Butterfly Tours Cycle Tour
One of the best ways to see the true Cambodia is on a cycling tour in the countryside. Take the "Off the Beaten Track" tour with Butterfly Tours Asia where you'll ride through the villages of Siem Reap, gaining insight into how rural Cambodians live their day-to-day life.

You'll embark on a 20-kilometer adventure over 4 hours with an English-speaking guide. You'll pass rice fields, lazy cows, Khmer villages and busy farmers. The locals who you'll meet along the way are very friendly and the children will be very excited to see you!

Pro Tip: Bring stickers = make friends with local kids

🎟️ **Budget:** $27
🌐 **Contact:** ButterflyTours.asia

Take a Cooking Class

What better way to learn about the traditions of Cambodia than through your stomach? Visit Lily's Secret Garden, a hygienic kitchen in an authentic teakwood style Cambodian house on stilts surrounded by a lush tropical garden. During your hour and a half cooking class, you'll be guided through a 3-course menu of traditional Khmer dishes using organic ingredients. Culinary experience is possibly the best Khmer souvenir to take home, don't ya think?

🌐 **Contact:** LilySecretGarden.com
💰 **Budget:** $24

📷 LILY SRECRET GARDEN

Kulen Nature Trails

Explore this maze of gorgeous rainforest trails in the mountains of Cambodia while stumbling upon ancient temples, respected monasteries, and rushing waterfalls. You'll walk along a gorgeous river and under cool, shady trees making for a much-needed escape from the heat. Once you reach the waterfall, there will be vendors selling snacks and beverages. Stock up and have a picnic under one of the pagodas next to the waterfall.

PRO TIP: It's best to visit the trails during the dry season. If you visit during the rainy season then your hike will be met with murky and muddy paths that just are no fun. Also, get a head start in the morning so that you don't run into other groups of tourists! You can find a guide for the Kulen Nature Trails by talking to a Tuk Tuk driver or asking your hotel.

CHAPTER 2: SIEM REAP

Shopping in Siem Reap

The Old Market
Get the local experience at The Old Market, or as the locals call it "Psar Chaa". Built in the 1920's, here is where residents of Siem Reap come to get their produce, grains, and meat for home cooked meals.

The market is divided into small sections selling different goods. Go to the fruit section where you can get organic Asian fruit at local prices, walk down the dim alleyways of the meat section where you'll find freshly made sausages hanging on strings, or walk through the rows of vendors sitting on straw floor mats selling dried seafood.

Open: Daily 7am-10pm
Where: Two Blocks South of Pub Street
Address: Psar Chaa Road

Angkor Night Market
Just a 2-minute walk from Pub Street, Angkor Night Market is a great place to do some drunk shopping. This night market has all of the quintessential Khmer handicrafts and artwork to take home like silk scarves, rings, wooden elephants- you know the drill. You'll also find lots of cute dresses, trek-worthy tank tops, and those cozy elephant pants (embrace them)!

Open: 5pm-12am
Where: North East of Pub Street

AHA's Fair Trade Village
At the AHA's Fair Trade Village, the money you spend goes directly towards the artists who sew, paint and carve all of the handicrafts sold. This non-profit market supports the local community by promoting a sustainable industry. Take home temple paintings, woven handbags, silk scarves, or delicate jewelry- rather than the mass-produced trinkets like you can find in the other markets.

Open: Monday - Friday 10am - 7pm
Where: On the road to the Temples ticket office
Address: Road 60, Trang Village, Sangkat Slorkram Commune Siem Reap

CHAPTER 2: **SIEM REAP**

Spas & Salons in Siem Reap

Lemongrass Garden
When you want the total spa treatment but don't want to spend half of your travel budget getting it, that's when you come to Lemongrass Garden. Just a couple dollars more than the common sub-par massage shops in the touristy areas, Lemongrass Garden is a professional experience that will leave you feeling positively pampered. They also offer manicures, body scrubs, facials, and waxing! Go for it.

Open: Daily 11am-11pm
Where: Near Pub Street
Address: 202, Sivatha Blvd, Krong Siem Reap

Street Foot Massages
For just a quick massage after a trek or before a long bus ride, just walk down Pub Street where massage chairs line the street, waiting for you to flop down. Get a foot massage with prices ranging from $1 for 15 minutes to $5 for an hour. These spots also offer oil massages and Khmer massages on the spot and are open late.

Open: Evening - Late
Where: Pub Street

Fish Spas
You might have seen them before- those clear aquariums full of fish with cozy chairs attached. But what are they for? The strangest pedicure of your life!

Stick your feet into the tank filled with fish that just love the taste of dead skin. They'll swarm your feet and nibble off those calluses you get from traveling and also, trim your dry cuticles in a matter of 20 minutes. It doesn't hurt but it totally tickles.

Have a wander on Walking Street where you'll find a handful of spas offering this service for around $3.

Open: Evening - Late
Where: Pub Street

CHAPTER 2: **SIEM REAP**

Nightlife in Siem Reap

Pub Street
Where the magic happens! Pub Street is the main attraction in Siem Reap once the sun goes down. With bright lights and music spilling out of bars and clubs until 4am, the road itself is worth a stroll. Lined with food trucks, clothing vendors, and beer specials, this is where travelers come to let their hair down and fill up on international cuisine. You can have a low key night here or get really wild depending on where you choose to drink. There are always Tuk Tuks waiting at the end of the road to take you home.

Temple Club
Sports fans! Come mingle with your brethren at this flat-screen lined sports bar on Pub Street. If there is a big match on, it will likely be playing. If you want to catch a specific game from home, connect with Temple Bar on Facebook and ask them to stream your team. When the game is over, you can head to the second floor to watch traditional Khmer dancers or head to the rooftop where you can melt into a bean bag chair to celebrate or mourn your team's success.

Open: Daily 10am-4am
Where: Pub Street

X Bar
Live music, fluorescent face paint, pool tables, a projector screen for the footy matches…oh and a half-pipe skate ramp on the roof: X Bar represents what is so fun about backpacking Asia. Back home, this place would never be up to code. Here, you can do whatever the hell you want. Buckets are cheap and so is the beer. It's impossible to not make a new friend here. (I can't bring myself to delete that rhyme).

⊙ **Open:** Daily 3pm-6am (Sunday closes at midnight)
📍 **Where:** East End of Pub Street

Khmer Pub Lane

You'll most likely see "Khmer Pub Lane" on Google Maps and get curious so I might as well give you the rundown now. This street is full of Karaoke Bars…aka prostitute bars. Guys come here to buy Khmer girls drinks, play pool, and take a girl home or into one of the "love hotels". If you are curious and want to peek into this world, then come take a walk or have an overpriced beer for the experience.

FUN FACT!

Angkor beer takes it name after Angkor Wat. Produced in Sihanoukville, it's Cambodia's national beer!

CHAPTER 2: **SIEM REAP**

How to Get Around Siem Reap

Walk
Put on some comfy shoes and go explore! This relatively small city is easy to navigate and difficult to get lost in.

NOTE: In the rainy season, roads are muddy. Don't wear anything too cute!

Tuk Tuk
Tuk Tuks are everywhere in Siem Reap! Expect to spend $1-5 to get anywhere in the city (depending on your haggling skills).

PRO TIP: As you walk around the city, Tuk Tuk drivers will be offering you tours or rides all day long. Hear one that has great English? Or see one with a genuine smile? Stop what you're doing and get their phone number. These guys are hard to find!

You don't need to make plans in the moment- but having a go-to Tuk Tuk driver will make your trip so much easier. These hard workers are just one call away when you need a ride.

Motorbike
For quick rides across the city or a ride home from the bars, you can hop on the back of a motorbike for 50 ¢ (2k Riel). You'll find these plainly-clothed dudes next to their motorbikes, usually hanging outside popular hotels and markets- waiting to give rides to tourists.

PRO TIP: While sketchy motorbike drivers are not usually a problem in Siem Reap, be cautious at night and choose to ride a Tuk Tuk driver rather than a lone man.

Rent a Bicycle

For around $2 a day, you can rent a bicycle and create your own city tour. Ride along the river, discover local restaurants down winding alleyways or take a map and go temple hunting.

Keep an eye out for guest houses that offer bikes for rent or visit thewhitebicycles.org for a list of places that rent bicycles with profits going to clean drinking water.

For Day Tours: Tuk Tuks & Taxis

Ready to explore Angkor Wat? Want to go on a tour of local villages? You can arrange your transportation right on the street with a Tuk Tuk driver.

Want a Taxi instead? Ask a Tuk Tuk driver to connect you with a Taxi Friend (they always have a friend!). Day tours in a Tuk Tuk usually cost around $18-$20 per day. Day tours in a Taxi can run anywhere from $25-$40

TRAVEL NOTES:

CHAPTER 2: SIEM REAP

How to Get to Siem Reap

Traveling internationally? There's an international airport in Siem Reap with daily flights from overseas and within Asia.

FROM PHNOM PENH

By Bus
There are tons of bus companies available in Cambodia- some are shit, break down often, and make a million stops. I always go with Giant Ibis, a trusted bus company with comfortable seats, air conditioning and wifi on board.

- **Point of Departure:** Giant Ibis Bus Terminal - Preah Moha Ksatreiyani Kossamak Ave (106)
- **When:** Daily @ 8:45 am, 9:45 am, 12:30 pm, 11 pm, 11:30 pm
- **Duration:** 5-6 Hours
- **Budget:** $15
- **Book:** www.12go.asia/en

By Private Taxi
- **Point of Departure:** Pick up at your hotel
- **When:** Whenever you want
- **Duration:** 4-5 hours
- **Budget:** $70-90
- **Book:** Facebook Group 'Taxi Share Cambodia'

By Plane
- **Point of Departure:** Phnom Penh Airport
- **When:** All day every day
- **Duration:** 45 Minutes
- **Budget:** $70+

By Boat
♥ Point of Departure: Minivan pick up from your hotel takes you to Sisowath Quay Port
⊙ When: During the months of July and March (when water levels are ideal) – everyday at 7am
⊙ Duration: 4 Hours
Budget: $18-$35 depending on the boat company
♥ Upon Arrival: The boat docks at the village of Chong Kneas, located about 12km (20-30 minutes) from Siem Reap. Take a $3 motorbike/tuk tuk ride from Chong Kneas to your hotel in Siem Reap.

PRO TIPS FOR THE BOAT:
♥ Only take the boat when the weather is bright and sunny!
♥ Buying tickets through a travel agency or your hotel is cheaper than buying at the dock.
♥ Bring snacks. Hell, bring meals.
♥ Avoid a company called Mekong Cruise

FROM BATTAMBANG

By Bus
On this route, only ride with a bus company called Capitol Tours. The other companies that drive this route are known to be sketchy AF.

♥ Point of Departure: Capitol Tours Office in Battambang
⊙ When: Daily – 7:45 am, 9:45 am, 1pm, 3pm
⊙ Duration: 3 hours
Budget: $5.50

FROM SIHANOUKVILLE

By Bus
This route is super long and bumpy, so I strongly suggest breaking up the journey with a stopover in Phnom Penh – but if you are hell bent on this idea, the night bus (aka sleeper bus) is an option.

9 Point of Departure: Minivan pick up at your hotel
When: Everyday 8:30pm
Duration: Roughly 12 hours
Budget: $15
Book: With any travel agent

By Plane
9 Point of Departure: Sihanoukville Airport
When: All day every day
Duration: 1 Hour
Budget: $100

PRO TIPS FOR SIEM REAP TRANSPORT
♥ Planes are small and bumpy! Expect these flights to have baggage fees, as well.
♥ Avoid a company called Virak Buntham
♥ Use companies called Sorya or GST

FROM THAILAND

By Bus
This long trip does include bathroom breaks and food stops, don't worry.

9 Point of Departure: Mo Chit Bus Terminal (Northern Bus Terminal)
When: Every hour between 5:30am and 10pm
Duration: 8-11 Hours (depending on weather, roads and traffic)
Budget: Around $30 USD

PRO TIPS
♥ Book with a company called 'Giant Ibis' for the most comfortable and reliable journey. This bus journey is pretty comfortable considering its long duration, the staff are professional, AND they hand out snacks and water during the trip.
♥ When you get to the border, you can leave your bags on the bus. You'll cross immigration and the bus will meet you on the other side. Check out the Visa and Immigration section on page 10 for more info on how this process works!

By Plane
♥ Point of Departure: Bangkok and Chiang Mai Airport
⊙ When: All day every day
⊙ Duration: 1 Hour
💵 Budget: $100

By Train
To ride in a 3rd class train with locals is such an amazing experience. You'll be crammed in a decently comfy seat with chickens and children sitting next to you. Reach out the window during stops to grab snacks from railway vendors. Take photos of rural life and soak up the beauty.

♥ Point of Departure: Hua Lamphong Railway Station
⊙ When: Everyday at 5:55am (there are more trains, but they won't get you across the border in 1 day)
⊙ Duration: 6 hour train – but a 12 hour journey (see below)
💵 Budget: $2 (amazing, right?)

IMPORTANT NOTE: The train's destination is to the border town of Aranyaprathet, which is a 10-minute Tuk Tuk ride to Cambodia's border, costing around 100 baht. The driver might try to take you to a "Visa Agency" – tell him you have an e-visa (even if you don't) and he'll take you to the border where you will walk out of Cambodia and into Cambodia.

From the Border in Aranyaprathet: After immigration, hop on the free 10-minute bus to Poipet Tourist Passenger International Terminal. The bus will be waiting for you, don't worry. At the terminal, your transport options to Siem Reap are as follows:
   → **Bus or Minivan** - $10
   → **Private Taxi** - $50

PRO TIP
♥ Don't let taxi drivers pressure you into their services by saying "the bus is full" or "the bus is leaving soon". In fact, the bus waits for passengers to fill up…which can take an hour.
♥ If you have the cash, take a taxi. Pay him half up front and half when you arrive at your hotel.

CHAPTER 2: SIEM REAP

From the Airport to Siem Reap

The Siem Reap airport is quite tiny! And surprisingly well organized for an operation of its size. This means that you can get in and out of the airport at lightning speed and can start the short 7km journey into town sooner rather than later.

Now, what to do once you're out of arrivals….

Option 1: Taxi on Arrival

Where: When you exit the airport, you'll see a taxi stand where you can arrange your ride.
Budget: $9 for a Van Taxi and $10 for a Regular Taxi (they run on price per meter + the car's size).

→ There are regular 4-person taxis and 6+ person taxi vans available.

Option 2: Tuk Tuk on Arrival

Siem Reap is full of Tuk Tuk drivers that go to and from the airport all day long. They do not work for the airport so you're able to get a cheaper rate.

Where: Walk outside of the airport and pass the taxi stand (ignoring anyone trying to sell you a taxi ride). Continue walking through the parking lot until you exit. There will be plenty of public tuk tuks waiting to give you a ride.
Budget: You can haggle your price between $4-6.

→ Tuk Tuks can fit up to 4 people – as long as you don't have an obscene amount of luggage.

PRO TIP: Any tuk tuk driver directly outside of the airport works for the airport. Their price will be higher and they have a reputation of always trying to sell you Angkor Wat Tours at an inflated price. They're fine for a 1-way journey. Just don't make further plans with them.

○ Option 3: Motorbike on Arrival
For just one person carrying a backpack, this is a cheap & fun option.

⚑ Where: The same spot where you'll find the tuk tuk drivers. Walk outside of the airport and pass the taxi stand (ignoring anyone trying to sell you a taxi ride). Continue walking through the parking lot until you exit. These guys are plainly dressed. Nothing to be alarmed by.
💵 Budget: You can haggle your price between $2-$4

PRO TIP: Don't wear your purse or handbag loosely as you ride- it can be snatched. Instead, wear it on the front of your body, across your chest.

○ Option 4: Arrange Pick-Up Before
Save yourself the hassle of explaining where you're going or haggling prices. Have transportation waiting for you at the airport.

❷ How: Ask your hotel about pick-up services or arrange pick-up with a local Tuk Tuk driver 1-2 days before.

💵 Budget: Hotels will usually charge around $7 or $8 while private Tuk Tuks charge $5 or $6.

FUN FACT!

Funerals in Cambodia are a big deal. They can last up to 49 days and cost up to $9,000 USD. And unlike most of the rest of the world, Cambodians wear white to mourn instead of black.

CHAPTER THREE

Battambang

📷 @ SMD.UNCORRUPTED.JPEG

CHAPTER THREE

Battambang

●────────●

Want to see old Cambodia? Before it was touched by the western world? Come to Battambang. While Battambang is the second largest city in Cambodia, it still isn't a destination that often makes it onto the traveler bucket list.

There are no white sand beaches or boozy pub crawls, but rather, Battambang is a city full of ancient temples, unspoiled local culture, and arguably some of the best Cambodian food in all the land.

Only about a 3-hour bus ride from Siem Reap, Battambang makes for a fun stop over before you head down to Phnom Penh. While it's a city of 250,000 people, it still has that small town charm that entices you to rent a bicycle or a moto and just explore.

Pack a backpack for the day and go on an excursion to discover side-of-the-road food stands, wander bright green rice fields, explore old country dirt roads, venture over to some ancient temples and then pop into a coffee shop for an artisan latte. Life here is slow and laid back- as most places worth seeing usually are.

CHAPTER 3: BATTAMBANG

Where to Stay in Battambang

Maisons Wat Kor

If it's good enough for Angelina Jole, it's good enough for you. Maisons Wat Kor is a rural guesthouse founded by a young boy who escaped the Khmer Rouge. Here, Cambodian traditions are kept alive with home cooked meals eaten together and hospitality that immerses you in Khmer culture. Not to mention, this hotel is stunning with teakwood architecture, lush gardens and a big blue pool!

★ *Style:* Private Rooms
Budget: $$$
Where: Wat Kor Village
Address: St. 800, Wat Kor Village

BOOK HERE

The Sanctuary Villa Battambang

Taking inspiration from a local Khmer Buddhist Temple, this hotel combines traditional décor with modern amenities to give guests a unique South East Asian vacation. Red tile roofs with dark teak wood accents next to sparkling water- everyday feels like waking up in a dream. If you do decide to leave the lap of luxury, guests can easily arrange day trips to nearby temples, or secure one of the in-house bicycles for private explorations. If you get hungry, the hotel's Oh Yeah! Restaurant offers Khmer, Thai and other international cuisines.

★ *Style:* Private Rooms + Villas
Budget: $$
Where: 15-minute ride from Bamboo Train Station, Battambang Bus and Boat Terminal
Address: No. 413, Chrey Village

BOOK HERE

La Villa

Art Deco, you say? Look no further because this little gem on the banks of the Sanker River will blow your mind. This beautiful guest house used to be an ancient colonial residence, which was then refurbished into a hotel. Each room comes with its own sitting area, free Wi-Fi, and other high-end amenities. If you ask ahead, you may even get a nice view of the pool from your hotel window. And with its convenient location in the city, it is easier to travel around Battambang's tourist destinations without any commuting hassle.

★ *Style:* Private Rooms
Budget: $$
Where: 5 to 7 hours from Phnom Phen, near Wat Kandal Temple
Address: N 185 Pom Romcheck 5, Sangkat Rattanak Krong

BOOK HERE

Battambang Dream Bungalows

The most comfortable homestay in Battambang! Live like a local and be close to nature- this place offers an all-around awesome experience. Guests can reserve 1 of 10 bamboo bungalows on site, fully equipped with the usual hotel amenities and a mosquito net for the evenings. Enjoy the stunning views of the mountains and relax into the lush greens surrounding the property. You never need to leave! Especially, because local dishes are served in the Dream Bungalow's restaurant daily.

★ *Style:* Private Bungalows
Budget: $
Where: 8KM from Psar Nat
Address: Kok Doung

BOOK HERE

CHAPTER 3: BATTAMBANG

Where to Eat in Battambang

HOC Café
This café has a very unique story that will pull at your heartstrings. The café is run by a NGO known as Hope of Children. They aid children across Cambodia who have been abused, orphaned and discriminated against, providing them with food, shelter, education and love. The café's staff are actually orphans from the NGO's orphanage. Their work in the restaurant is helping them to become independent and earn money for their future. The café offers scrumptious Khmer and Japanese-style breakfast, lunch and dinner sets for a reasonable price.

Open: Tuesdays to Sundays 8am – 2pm/ 5pm – 10pm
Address: No. 205-207, Group 38, Maphey Ousaphea Village

Smokin' Pot
Craving Cambodian flavors? Check out Smokin' Pot where the food is homemade, using traditional pots, pans, and cookware. This gem of a restaurant offers both Asian and vegetarian meals that are to die for. Smokin' Pot also offers cooking lessons for anyone interested to learn some of the restaurant's best sellers under the teachings of the head chef and owner Vannak. At the end of each lesson, students would even get a copy of the restaurant's recipes to take home.

Open: Daily 9am – 11pm
Address: 229, Group 8, 20 Ouspehea Village

Jaan Bai Restaurant
Rice bowls anyone? Literally meaning 'rice bowls' in Khmer, Jaan Bai offers a variety of dishes that cater to everyone's taste buds. At least half of the

menu is vegan, making this a must-try restaurant for fresh Asian and Khmer vegetarian favorites. Every ingredient used in the restaurant is certified fresh and locally sourced. Customers can even check out the open kitchen to see how meals are prepared.

Open: Daily 11am – 10pm (last order at 9pm)
Address: Corner 2 Street and 1 ½ Street

Nary Kitchen
One of the most popular restaurants in town! This family restaurant opened in 2009 and is a favorite amongst locals and tourists alike looking for traditional Cambodian cuisine. All the ingredients used by the restaurant are bought fresh daily. When you visit, be sure to try out the restaurant's most famous dishes: the Fish Amok and Lok Lak. PS: Nary's Kitchen also offers cooking lessons for an affordable price!

Open: Daily 8am – 10pm (Closing time often depends on how busy they get!)
Address: No 650, 111 Street

Ambrosia Café
Ambrosia Café is a vegetarian's paradise as their menu features a huge selection of vegetarian and vegan dishes. All of the food served in this café are MSG free, ensuring healthy meals for every order. They also offer a nice selection of drinks for customers, locally sourced and made from fresh ingredients. While eating, you can use the restaurant's fast WiFi to share photos of the restaurant's soothing décor . Or put your phone down to play some board games with your friends.

Open: Daily 9am- 11pm
Address: 20 Usaphea Village

HUMAN Gallery - Joseba Etxebarria Photography

An artist and a humanist, Joseba Etxebarria has created a truly extraordinary art gallery concept here in Battambang. Visit his gallery to see breathtaking portraits of people from all around the world. Kick your feet up and have a freshly roasted cup of coffee along as you take it all in.

BONUS: When you visit this gallery, you are contributing to a well-deserving local NGO called Wings for the Future. 20% of sales of the coffee & art pieces go towards bettering the lives of extremely impoverished children living in Boeng Raing, a community just north of Battambang. Mr. Etxebarria is often hanging around the gallery and is extremely welcoming in discussion about his project!

Open: Monday to Saturday 10am – 2pm/ 4pm – 9pm
Address: Across the road from White Rose Restaurant

TRAVEL NOTES:

CHAPTER 3: **BATTAMBANG**

Sights & History in Battambang

Visit the Well of Shadows
As you first approach the Well of Shadows, it might look like another beautiful golden pagoda with spirals reaching towards the sky. But look a little closer and you'll see that this pagoda serves a deeper purpose.

The Well of Shadows stands to memorialize the lives brutally lost during the Khmer Rouge. This monument is not for the faint of heart, as you'll be greeted by human skulls and bones – many with visible gunshot holes- encased in a large glass box. Below them are relics depicting the horrors that took place during this dark time, including torture and killings.

To get there, ride your bicycle or motorbike along the east side of the Sangkar River and you'll meet the Well of Shadows approximately 6 kilometers north of Battambang.

The Killing Field at Wat Samrong Knong
It's a disgrace that happened all over the country. The Khmer Rouge took the most sacred grounds and turned them into killing fields. Wat Samrong Knong is no different.

This pristine temple in Battambang is one of the oldest in the province. Built in 1707, this temple is unlike others that you've seen as it has been built with an unusual combination of cement, brick, and wood. A marriage of materials so fascinating that you could study it for hours.

Unfortunately, that isn't all there is to see here. There is a monument to pay respect to the some 10,000 Cambodians that lost their lives here during the senseless genocide during the Khmer Rouge.

IMPORTANT NOTE: Buddhist monks are present at this temple, so it's important to dress modestly.

Visit Banan Temple
It's such a surreal experience to visit this Angkorian temple with overgrown green jungle vines nestled up a set of eroding brick stairs in the middle of nowhere.

Built at the end of the 12th century, it's a miracle that these structures are still standing. Make your way up the steps of steep stairs leading to a platform with 5 separate buildings that make up this temple. From the temple, you can see gorgeous views of the Sangker River, palm tree forests, and farming fields of green rice paddies. On clear days, you can also get a view of the crocodile-shaped mountain to the south.

There will be lots of vendors, beggars, and locals selling religious handicrafts along the way.

FUN FACT!

There are around 4,000 documented temples in Cambodia. However, it is believed that there are many more buried deep in the jungle that haven't been discovered yet!

Hike to the Killing Cave

Tie your sneakers up tight and head off on the gorgeous mountain trail where monkeys wander, birds sing, and swarms of bats fly overhead at sunset. You'll pass peaceful pagodas, monuments, and statues- all leading to a starkly different memorial.

Once you eventually reach the caves, prepare yourself to learn about the horrors that plagues this area during the Khmer Rouge's reign of terror. As you descend into the cave, you'll notice the contrast between natural beauty and manmade horror. Once inside, you'll be greeted by a museum of human bones lining the perimeter of the cave.

Look above through the skylight. This is where the Khmer Rouge murdered innocent families and scholars, by pushing their bodies to fall into the very cave in which you are standing.

See the Kampong Pil Pagoda

The adventure starts before you even arrive at Kampong Pil Pagoda. First, you'll have to cross the long bamboo suspension bridge built over a flowing river which swings with every step. Move aside when daring locals ride their motorbike across and hold on tight.

Once you reach the pagoda, your heart might be racing a bit. A calm wander around the premises is enough to take you back to a peaceful state. A traditional pagoda with a golden roof and white walls, Kampon Pil is totally picturesque. What makes this pagoda unique, however, are the Buddha statues, the Angkorian people sculptures, and the massive reclining Buddha on site. It's a colorful place with cheerful energy and lots of photo opportunities!

CHAPTER 3: BATTAMBANG

Fun Things to Do in Battambang

Ride the Bamboo Train
While Cambodia did have the best intentions of having a fully functioning railway system, they just couldn't seem to make it happen. The slow trains lacked efficiency and speed, therefore, many train services were suspended in 2009, leaving most of the tracks abandoned.

But if there's one thing you should know about the Khmer people, it's that they are innovative beyond belief. So it's no surprise that they took those abandoned tracks and created their own transport system.

By building mini boat-sized bamboo trains that fit a small family, locals created a way to easily transport people and goods far distances. These "trains" run manually with a lever and must be taken off the tracks any time two trains encounter one another. It's a silly system that actually works.

Sip at a Winery
Prasat Phnom Banon Winery is your chance to taste a variety of wine like you'll find no place else. Cambodia's only winery, this unique vineyard grows their very own organic grapes to make some unique blends. They grow shiraz and cabernet sauvignon grapes that produce incredible reds. This Battambang Winery also grows a special genus of Black Queen and Black Opal grapes to make a bubbly rose.

Kayak through Villages and Countryside
The riverside of Battambang is where many locals have set up houses. The neighborhoods consist of a collection of houses built on stilts in the water. The locals use this water for everything: to fish, swim, and wash their clothes. And to boat for transportation.

During your kayak adventure, you'll pass these houses as you go downstream into the countryside. There you'll kayak along rice fields as you see farmers busy at work and pass dense rainforests giving off a cool breeze.

Rent your kayaks through Green Orange Kayaks, a NGO school who uses the proceeds to fund the local children's education. Your tour will include steady kayaks, paddles, life jackets, and a friendly English speaking guide. Contact: Green Orange Kayaks

Battambang Circus

Support student artists by joining the audience at Phare Ponleu Selpak, Battambang's lively local circus! Unlike other circuses that get bad reputations for exploiting people and animals, this circus is exactly the opposite! In fact, Phare Ponleu Selpak is run by a Cambodian NGO that takes street kids and youth from rough backgrounds, and gives them a chance to learn new forms of art to express themselves and make a living.

The circus performance is full of excitement. There are Angkorian-era dances, acrobatic artists, mind-blowing jugglers, and more. The show is put on only two nights a week, so make sure to schedule this incredible evening ahead of time.

♥ Check out **Phare Ponleu Selpak** on Facebook

PHARE PONLEU SELPAK

Shopping in Battambang

Phsar Nath Market
Battambang's most recognizable and central landmark is the Phsar Nath Market- otherwise known as the Central Market. Built in the 1930's by French architects, this market has a distinct design that sets it apart from all other buildings in the area. You'll find French style shop fronts and opulent ceilings that you certainly wouldn't expect to find in small-city Cambodia.

The market serves as the main hub for locals to buy and sell all sorts of produce. Like most Cambodian markets, you'll find wet sections with fresh fish and hanging raw meat, and dry sections with fresh fruit and dried seafood. There are lots of flavors, smells, and sights to be taken in. Go in the morning to see the peak of the excitement!

🕓 **Open:** Before dawn-midnight
🏛 **Address:** Where Street 3 and Street 113 meet

Jewel in the Lotus
You like weird? Eclectic? Vintage? Putting an Asian spin on your favorite genres of unique and rare trinkets is this hole in the wall shop in Battambang. You'll find antique clothing from neighboring South East Asian countries, old school photos of Cambodia, Buddhist charms, and propaganda posters. It's like The Good Will but cool.

🕓 **Open:** When they feel like it
🏛 **Address:** 76 Street 2.5, Battambang

CHAPTER 3: BATTAMBANG

How to Get to Battambang

FROM SIEM REAP

By Bus
- **Point of Departure:** Capitol Guesthouse near Orussey Market
- **When:** Daily 8am & 2pm
- **Duration:** 3 Hours
- **Budget:** Around $7 USD
- **Book:** BookMeBus.com

By Private Taxi
- **Point of Departure:** Pick up from your hotel
- **When:** Whenever you want
- **Duration:** 2.5 Hours
- **Budget:** $40-50 USD
- **Book:** BookMeBus.com

By Boat
Listen…this boat has 0 safety standards. They overload it with passengers and cargo. Fair warning, just in case a travel agency tries to make it sound like a luxury cruise!

- **Point of Departure:** Pick up from your hotel
- **When:** 7am
- **Duration:** 8-10 Hours
- **Budget:** $22 USD

Ps. You can book the entire boat for $180 which will be much safer than traveling with the whole village.

FROM PHNOM PENH

By Bus
♥ Point of Departure: Capitol Guesthouse near Orussey Market
⊙ When: Daily 7 am, 8 am, 9 am, 10:30 am, 11:30 am, 12:30 pm, 1 pm, 2:15 pm, 2:45 pm, 4 pm, 5:30 pm
⊙ Duration: 5-7 Hours
💰 Budget: Around $8 USD

By Minivan
♥ Point of Departure: Pick up from your hotel
⊙ When: Daily 5:30 am, 6:20 am, 7:30 am, 8:30 am, 11:30 am, 12:30 pm, 1:30 pm, 2:30 pm (depending on the company)
⊙ Duration: 5-6 Hours
💰 Budget: Around $8 USD

By Private Taxi
♥ Point of Departure: Pick up from your hotel
⊙ When: Whenever you want
⊙ Duration: 4 Hours
💰 Budget: Around $60 USD
🌐 Book: Visit the Facebook group 'Cambodia Taxi Share'

FUN FACT!

Tokay geckos are considered to be lucky in Cambodia. If there's one near to you and it calls out its distinctive chirp more than 7 times that means you're lucky!

CHAPTER FOUR

Kampot

BOUDEWIJN HUYSMANS

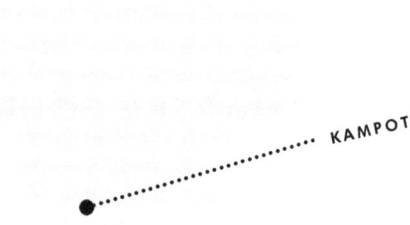

CHAPTER FOUR

Kampot

The sleepy town of Kampot isn't trying to be anything it's not. Naturally beautiful and effortlessly enchanting, you'll slip right into a balance of laid back days on the river and scenic drives over red dirt roads.

Relatively untouched by mainstream tourism, its natural beauty puts you on the fast-track to getting back in touch with Mother Earth via rock climbing, river tours, and expeditions into the jungle.

However…Kampot has a thriving community of expats who live here. Kampot is the very first place I come to spend a week or so whenever I visit Cambodia.

Kampot also has a rich history as it served as the capital city under French rule. Today, travelers can hop on a motorbike and explore handfuls of abandoned French colonial mansions and churches reminiscent of Indiana Jones-style voyages.

All in all, Kampot is unlike any other Cambodian city you'll find. If you like natural adventure, historical discoveries and a vibrant expat community, don't skip over this hidden gem of a city.

AREAS TO EXPLORE IN KAMPOT

There's more than meets the eye when it comes to exploring the tiny town of Kampot.

Kampot Town
Bus stations, pharmacies, hostels, clothing shops, motorbike rentals, western & Khmer restaurants…it's all condensed into a small city center with bustling traffic. You'll often hear people give directions using "The Durian" roundabout as a point of reference.

The Other Side of the River
…as the locals call it. There are a couple bridges (one for cars and one for motorbikes) that stretch over to the more jungley side of Kampot. Over here, you'll find lots of lazy riverside guesthouses, a few yummy restaurants, and Bokor Mountain.

@ARITRAROYS

CHAPTER 4: **KAMPOT**

Where to Stay in Kampot

Kampot is still pretty off the grid. That being said, addresses aren't really a thing over here. When you arrive in Kampot, you can tell your driver or Tuk Tuk driver the name of the place where you're staying and they'll get you there one way or another.

Karma Traders

BOOKING.COM

Confession: Karma Traders is my second home in Cambodia. The epicenter of a warm and friendly expat social circle, you are always welcome to pull up a stool at the bar and join in on the positive vibes and weird conversation. This place has never known a stranger.

There is a brand new social swimming pool on site, rooftop bar with serene sunset views over Bokor Mountain, cozy guest rooms and dorms for rest, and a collection of furry animals to be cuddled. How can you pass this up?

Try to schedule your visit to fall on Taco Tuesday where amazing musicians from around the world play as you feast on some seriously impressive tacos. Not around on Tuesdays? No worries. Enjoy happy hour everyday from 5-7pm.

PS. Show the bartenders your copy of this book and get 1 free Joss Shot on Alexa's tab!

★ **Style:** Dorms & Privates
Budget: $
Where: Kampot Town

BOOK HERE

Meraki

I've just booked a week-long stay at Meraki as a peaceful and serene place to write my new book. Meraki is a gorgeous riverside garden paradise with tropical flowers and plants surrounding simple, thatched-roof bungalows. Lounge in a hammock while you watch small-engine boats tug by on the water or play a game of pool with a draft beer in hand. Here is where problems melt away and inspiration flows. Ps. These guys are super 420 friendly, if you're into that sort of thing.

★ **Style:** Privates
Budget: $
Where: The Other Side of the River

BOOK HERE

Hotel Five.S

Right in the center with a pool. You get the whole goose when you stay at Hotel Five.S. Each room has its own tropical garden, a unique open-air bathroom, a heavenly bed, and a fully stocked bathroom with lovely smelling soaps and shampoos. Up your budget just a bit for a private balcony overlooking the city. Perfect for a bottle of wine to finish off a relaxing Kampot vacation.

★ **Style:** Privates
Budget: $$
Where: Kampot Town - Walkable!

BOOK HERE

Nary Garden

Imagine bamboo bungalows with thatched roofs in the jungle next to the river. This place is rustic and homey. Your bungalow is simple with just a bed on the floor and a mosquito net up above. Pass out here but spend your time wandering the property, having lunch overlooking the river where fish swim by and life moves slowly. If you're wanting a true, authentic Cambodian experience while still being comfortable - don't hesitate.

★ **Style:** Privates
Budget: $
Where: Off the Beaten Path

BOOK HERE

Retro Kampot Guesthouse

All you need to be happy is a hammock on a balcony overlooking the river. I love staying here because it's a balance between jungle life and city life. You can stay in a more modern "apartment" where you have A/C and a bed not just sitting on the ground - but you've still got the jungle ambiance! Go explore on your free kayak and then come back to incredible food at the on-site restaurant!

★ **Style:** Privates
Budget: $
Where: The Green Loop

BOOK HERE

"The real voyage of discovery consists not in seeking new landscapes, but in having new eyes."

— MARCEL PROUST

CHAPTER 4: **KAMPOT**

Where to Eat in Kampot

Karma Traders Kampot
Schedule your Kampot trip to fall on a Tuesday for the tastiest Taco Tuesday ever. Every week, Karma Traders serves up the best tacos in town- almost always selling out by the end of the night. Choose between 7hr Slow-cooked Coca-Cola Pulled Pork, Paprika Shredded Chicken, and Tender Spiced Pumpkin fillings served with fresh pico de gallo, crunchy coleslaw, spicy pineapple salsa, Tapatio mayo and lime. $2 each or $5 for 3. Pair with a tasty cocktail or ice cold beer from the tap. Pure bliss.

🕒 **Open:** Every day from 8am to late
📍 **Where:** Kampot Town

Epic Arts Café
Get your coffee fix and contribute to a well-deserving cause at this NGO run café and art gallery. Epic Arts Café aims to increase work opportunities for disabled people in Kampot and generates revenue to put towards local art programs. You'll find that many of the staff here are deaf, so go ahead and order by ticking the boxes on your menu or take a shot at some basic Cambodian Sign Language.

The humanitarian mission is just the cherry on top of some really REALLY good food. I've never had a meal here that didn't blow me away. Try the Banana & Coconut Pancakes, Mango Salad with Grilled Tuna, or Bacon Paninis.

🕒 **Open:** Everyday 7:30 am - 5:00 pm
📍 **Where:** Kampot Town near the Old Market
🏠 **Address:** #67 Oosaupia Muoy

Magic Sponge

Huge sandwiches. Tacos. Eggs benedict. Classic breakfasts. Magic Sponge has the comfort food you crave, plus awesome hospitality from owners who have been food heroes in this town for years. They've often got fun events going on like movie nights, pub quiz nights and even taco tuesdays. Check them out on Facebook to see what they've got going on next.

◉ **Open:** Everyday 7:30 am - 8:30 pm (closes at 2pm on Sundays)
Address: Street 730 (Guesthouse Street)
f Facebook: Magic Sponge

Twenty Three

Never trust a massive menu. Rather, you want to look for the charming restaurants with small menus, where each dish is executed with complete and utter perfection. And that's exactly what you'll find here at Twenty Three, the gourmet gastro pub in Kampot. Serving Charcuterie Boards, braised pork belly, lamb shanks, fresh tuna - if it wasn't for the $10 price tags, you'd have thought you were dining in a Michelin star restaurant…

◉ **Open:** Wednesday-Monday 5:30am-9:30pm (closed on Tuesday)
Where: Kampot Town near the river
Address: 23 East Street

Tertúlia

Seeking seafood Portuguese style? The culinary geniuses at Tertúlia have taken advantage of the fish, snails, squid and shellfish in the region to create gorgeous dishes right here in Kampot. Try the Tuna Tartare or the Tiger Prawns with Kampot Peppers – and treat yourself to a glass of red wine. Don't worry, with dishes averaging around $7, you can definitely afford it.

◉ **Open:** Tuesday to Friday 5pm – 11pm & Saturday 12 pm - 11pm
Where: Just over the New Bridge
Address: Tuek Chhu Road

CHAPTER 4: **KAMPOT**

Things to Do in Kampot

Be Lazy
Kampot is the best place in Cambodia for girls looking to sit next to a mellow river with a good book, cold beer, and laid back vibes. You'll find handfuls of guest houses filled with chilled out people looking to do the same. PS. Kampot's guest houses are very 420 friendly, if you're into that sort of thing.

Drive to Bokor National Park
Bokor National Park offers more than just thick jungle, singing birds, and babbling brooks; it is also home to massive abandoned French Colonial houses and churches, giving this jungle an eerie, ghost town vibe. You'll experience all of this on your drive up, and then at the top of the mountain, you'll be met with a towering statue of Buddha overlooking insanely beautiful views of winding valleys and farmland. If you're comfortable on a motorbike, this is the ideal way to explore; if not, hire a tuk tuk or ask your hotel about hiring a minivan.

📷 @ ARITRAROYS

Explore the Local Villages via Motorbike

Some of the most rewarding days spent in Kampot are the days where you just point yourself in a general direction and drive. Head towards Nut Hill (Phnom Dung), Fishing Island (Koh D'tray), or Kampot's salt fields to immerse yourself in some incredible scenery.

You'll drive past small shops offering bottles of petrol and cans of beer, as well as local restaurants serving authentic Cambodian dishes and friendly company from the locals. The roads are a bit bumpy so it's best you go one person per bike!

Go Paddle Boarding

The mellow surface of the Kampot River is the ideal place for a day of paddle boarding. No worries if you don't have any experience as a local company called SUP Asia offers paddle boarding lessons in the most ideal environment for learning.

Take the board out for an hour or two where you'll paddle down the river surrounded by birds and wildlife, and hop off the board into the water for a refreshing swim. If you're up for a real adventure, SUP Asia offers 2-3 day excursions where you paddle into local fishing villages and get a real taste for Cambodian culture.

La Plantation Pepper Farm

Fun Fact: Kampot's #1 export is black pepper! Foodies will love the opportunity to tour black pepper farms where guides walk you through various stages of black pepper forests, and let you sample the spicy products along the way. Best of all, the tours are free of charge without any pushy people trying to make a sale!

After the short tour, take a seat in the on-site restaurant where you can dine on some extremely fresh dishes with black pepper right off the vine. Of course, there are bags of black pepper to purchase at local prices as souvenirs.

Kayak on the River

Depending on where you're renting, you can become a pioneer of the 30-kilometer Kampot River on your very own kayak for as little as $3.50 an hour. There are tons of guesthouses and shops around Kampot that offer kayak tours and kayaks for your own explorations.

Visit Green Orange Bungalows or Meraki who will help you map out the ideal kayaking route to include mangroves, rapids, bird watching and peaceful views.

Get a Tattoo

It's a right of passage to get a tattoo from Mathilda, the mother of tattoos here in the south of Cambodia. A French expat who showed up on Koh Rong 5 years ago, barely speaking English, she is now a staple in the community. Become a part of the Cambodia family with an ultra feminine, spiritual, or minimalistic tattoo that will forever remind you of your journey in South East Asia. Don't be surprised if you bump into other people in the world with Mathilda tattoos – we're everywhere!

Where: Find her tattoo shop at Karma Traders
Contact: Facebook- Mathilda Tattoos in Kampot

Rock Climbing

If you like extreme sports that defy gravity, why not take a shot at rock climbing in Cambodia? The climbing pros at Climbodia will guide you as you embark on a 35-meter top rope climb to reach a cliff side summit with amazing views of salt flats, Bokor Mountain, and on a clear day, as far as Phu Quoc in Vietnam.

Not wild enough? Climbodia also offers abseiling tours where you drop down 30 meters into a hole in the earth with only a head lamp to guide the way. Tours are available all year round, run for approximately 4 hours and are a bargain at around $40.

Take a Scenic Drive to Kep
25km east from Kampot is Kep, a quaint beachside town that is a foodie heaven. Rent a motorbike and take the easy scenic drive down the highway. The ride to Kep is a comfortable journey, even for beginners, as the traffic isn't too overwhelming and the directions are literally straightforward.

When you reach Kep, park your bike and kick your feet up in one of the many hammock filled gazebos. Food hawkers will come to you selling the famous Kampot Pepper Crab and cold beverages. Afterwards, have a walk around the small seaside market where fresh fish are grilled and dried squid are sold on a stick.

Hang Out in your Bathing Suit
Have a pool day at Karma Traders, lounge in an inner tube on the river at Naga House or slide until your bum is bruised at Arcadia Water Park & Guest House. You don't have to be a guest- just a patron who buys drinks and/or food.

Organize a Date with Nature
✷ Watch the sunset on the river with Lazy Day River Tours
✷ From the riverside, watch the fishing boats head out to sea at sunset
✷ Spectacular bird watching in the evenings from the balcony at Paris Guesthouse 1 - next to Mr. Chims

☾ KAMPOT NIGHTLIFE

This sleepy town doesn't have a huge party scene, rather, you'll find a handful of guest houses that throw live music nights, themed parties or a steady flow of low-key boozing.

Ask around for what's going on each night - but you can count on one party every week that is an absolute must:

☉ **Tuesday:** Taco Tuesday & Live Music at Karma Traders – 6:30 pm

CHAPTER 4: **KAMPOT**

Shopping in Kampot

Kampot Night Market
Head towards "The Big Durian" roundabout where you'll find stall after stall of clothing, shoes, hammocks, souvenirs, and more. You could easily spend a couple hours just roaming around and practicing your haggling skills.

Once you've worked up an appetite, get your eat on with grilled Khmer delicacies on a stick, noodle soup, beef sandwiches, mango sticky rice and of course, cold beer. There are plastic tables and chairs where you can chill out with your crew, taking your time as you go and picking dishes at random to create the perfect spread.

⊙ **Open:** Everyday 8am-10pm
Where: Kampot Town
Address: Near the Durian Roundabout

TRAVEL NOTES:

....

....

....

....

CHAPTER 4: KAMPOT

How to Get Around Kampot

Rent a Motorbike
If and only if you're comfortable on a motorbike, go ahead and rent one. Traffic in the center of Kampot can be a little hectic but once you're in the mountains and the "other side of the river", motorbikes are the best way to really soak up everything Kampot has to offer.

Rent a Bicycle
Many guest houses have bicycles for rent or know where you can find one. Bicycles are great for exploring the flat city, just keep in mind that traffic is fast-paced so try to keep to the shoulder and give yourself plenty of time when crossing busy intersections. Drivers won't slow down for you.

Tuk Tuk
When you need to get from your guesthouse to a bar or restaurant, have reception ring you a Tuk Tuk. Prices are usually $1-5 per person depending on where you're going and how many people you've got.

Walk
Staying in Kampot Town? It's easy to get around on your own two feet. Walk along the riverside or explore the side streets full of small businesses and shops.

CHAPTER 4: **KAMPOT**

How to Get to Kampot

FROM PHNOM PENH

By Bus
- **Point of Departure:** Giant Ibis Bus Terminal
- **When:** Daily at 8am and 2:45pm
- **Duration:** 2.5 hours
- **Budget:** $15
- **Book:** www.12go.asia/en

By Private Taxi
- **Point of Departure:** Pick up at your hotel
- **When:** Whenever you want
- **Duration:** 3 hours
- **Budget:** $40
- **Book:** Check out our section called 'Driver Directory' on page 225.

By Train
- **Point of Departure:** Phnom Penh Railway Station
- **When:** Friday at 3pm, Saturday at 7am, Sunday at 7 am, Monday at 4pm
- **Duration:** 4-5 hours
- **Budget:** $6

FROM SIHANOUKVILLE

By Minibus
- **Point of Departure:** Minivan pick up at your hotel
- **When:** Multiple times per day
- **Duration:** 2 hours
- **Budget:** $6-10

By Private Taxi
- **Point of Departure:** Pick up at your hotel
- **When:** Whenever you want
- **Duration:** 2 hours
- **Budget:** $30+
- **Book:** Check out our section called 'Driver Directory' on page 225.

Crime & Safety in Kampot

Crime
Only recently has petty crime made an appearance in the town of Kampot. It's the same old story: motorbike drivers might try to snatch your purse as you ride or walk alongside them. Sketchy hostels might magically swallow up belongings left unattended in bathrooms, dorm rooms, or left out on bar counters. Keep your valuables close and stay at trusted hostels and guesthouses.

Safety
Motorbike accidents are common in Cambodia with both travelers and locals. Always wear a helmet and close-toed shoes (no flip flops) and be extra cautious while riding at night.

CHAPTER FIVE

Sihanoukville

📷 @ANNEAWAY

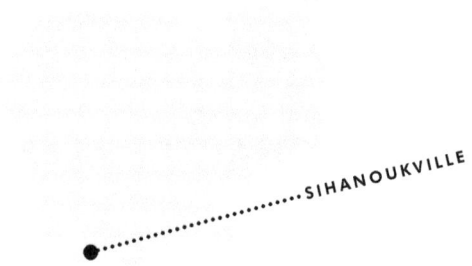

CHAPTER FIVE

Sihanoukville

The sleepy town of Kampot isn't trying to be anything it's not. Naturally beautiful and effortlessly enchanting, you'll slip right into a balance of laid back days on the river and scenic drives over red dirt roads.

Relatively untouched by mainstream tourism, its natural beauty puts you on the fast-track to getting back in touch with Mother Earth via rock climbing, river tours, and expeditions into the jungle.

However…Kampot has a thriving community of expats who live here. Kampot is the very first place I come to spend a week or so whenever I visit Cambodia.

Kampot also has a rich history as it served as the capital city under French rule. Today, travelers can hop on a motorbike and explore handfuls of abandoned French colonial mansions and churches reminiscent of Indiana Jones-style voyages.

All in all, Kampot is unlike any other Cambodian city you'll find. If you like natural adventure, historical discoveries and a vibrant expat community, don't skip over this hidden gem of a city.

AREAS TO EXPLORE IN SIHANOUKVILLE

Serendipity Beach (Ochheuteal Beach)
Nestled right next to the main boat pier, you'll find Serendipity Beach lined with a cement boardwalk/path. All along the boardwalk, there are beachfront restaurants and shady umbrella stands to match. This boardwalk is getting busier and busier but the beach shacks aren't able to accommodate the influx of travelers. So if you decide to come here for the day, come for the people watching and experiencing, rather than the "toes in the sand" vacation vibes.

…I'm really selling it, aren't I?

Otres 1
More aimed towards backpackers, this beach offers tons of budget options with cheap rooms and dorms.

Otres 2
Otres 2 offers the posh life with upscale resorts, swimming pools with a view, and fantastic service.

Sihanoukville City
Wild, busy and full of chaos! But…there is a KFC.

@SIMKIMHORT

CHAPTER 4: SIHANOUKVILLE

Where to Stay in Sihanoukville

I don't recommend staying in Sihanoukville unless your transportation schedule forces you to. And if it does…you'll actually have a great time (there are just better places to be). That being said, there are two places I recommend you stay in Sihanoukville.

Onederz Sihanoukville

Onederz Hostel has three very appealing traits that other dorms in Sihanoukville just don't offer: social pool, fast internet & sparkling clean rooms with brand new beds. On top of that, the location is fabulous! You're just a 10-minute walk to the beach and a 3-minute walk to all the best restaurants and bars. As a fairly new brand, the staff are freshly trained and enthusiastic to help you plan your trip! Female dorms available!

★ **Style:** Dorms
Budget: $
Where: At the top of Serendipity Road
Address: Golden Lion Traffic Circle

BOOK HERE

Sunset Lounge

Have it all: the party and the sleep! Put on a breezy dress, take off your shoes, and melt into this modern, chic cocktail bar and big ass pool. Located under big billowing trees right next to the beach! Each room is quaint and charming with its own terrace and hammock. Next to everything: the ferry, the parties, the beach; but tucked away from the hustle and bustle of the city!

★ **Style:** Privates
Budget: $$
Where: Ochheuteal Beach

BOOK HERE

CHAPTER 4: **SIHANOUKVILLE**

Where to Eat in Sihanoukville

Khmer Food on the Beach
Serendipity Beach is lined with fresh seafood displays chilling on ice and menus filled with classic Khmer dishes. Cooked to order, you eat with your toes in your sand, a cold beer in your hand, and some fantastic people watching (sorry that didn't rhyme with sand or hand).

Just head towards the pier and hang a left on the beach and follow your senses!

☾ SHHANOUKVILLE NIGHTLIFE

Serendipity Beach
At night, the boardwalk comes alive with loud music, flashing lights, and a younger crowd of both travelers and Cambodians who love to party. Walking around the main road, you'll be approached by barefoot bartenders passing out free drink coupons for JJs or other beachfront clubs. This is how they fill that place up night after night during high season!

Pro Tip: Be sure to watch your purse and pockets! The cute little beggar kids roaming around the beach are quite skilled with the elusive bag snatch..

CHAPTER 4: **SIHANOUKVILLE**

Shopping in Sihanoukville

Phsar Leu Market
Step into the shoes of local Cambodians at this massive flea market in Sihanoukville. Tucked in the center of town is a large plaza filled with nearly 100 vendors selling a variety of goods. You'll find stalls selling children's clothing, stalls with bathing suits, stalls for gold watches and jewelry, and of course, stalls with lots of food.

The outside perimeter of the market is bustling with locals who have come to pick up fruit, veg, and bread to feed their whole family- it's quite a hectic scene to watch. Sample local delicacies like jackfruit or the infamous stinky Durian. Just watch your toes as spikey produce is strewn about!

♥Where: Sihanoukville Town

Shops along Serendipity Road
Wander the main road that leads down to Serendipity Beach. You'll find plenty of reasonably priced clothing stores selling beachy cover-ups and flowy dresses. You can also buy electronics, DVDs, iPods with music loaded to go, purses made from recycled materials, sunglasses, postcards and my favorite…snacks to stuff in your purse for later.

♥Where: Serendipity Road

CHAPTER 4: **SIHANOUKVILLE**

Things to Do in Sihanoukville

Go on an Island Hopping Tour

Don't have time to stay on all the islands? Visit them all in one day with Otres Island Hopper Tours. For $20, you get an incredible ocean adventure where you'll snorkel in crystal clear water with colorful fish and stop off at some of the most gorgeous beaches that you've ever seen! Your tour includes lunch, snorkeling gear, water and beer!

PRO TIP: During high season, it is possible to ask the tour boat to drop you off at Koh Ta Kiev for 1 or 2 nights. You'll hop back on their boat when they visit next. 2 birds with 1 stone!

CHECK IT OUT: Pop into any tour office or ask at your hotel. The same few tours are offered everywhere!

Kbal Chhay Waterfall

Head out to Kbal Chhay Waterfall and let the fresh water streams cool you down under the hot Cambodian sun. Rest beneath the falls for a vigorous back massage and lay down in the revitalizing pools of water as crystal streams rush over your body.

When you're ready to dry off, there are traditional Khmer bamboo huts to provide some shade. Swing in a sturdy hammock and picnic on the straw mats below you. There will be hawkers selling snacks and beverages as you cross the bamboo bridge to help you stock up!

ὄ *How to get there:* Hire a Tuk Tuk!

Go Sailing

Sail Sihanoukville has mini catamarans for rent! These small white boats with bright green sails line the beach on Otres and are hard to miss! You don't have to be a sailing expert or be experienced in sailing at all to have a catamaran adventure in Sihanoukville. You can go out on a relaxing ride where you'll take in gorgeous views of the shore or sign up for sailing lessons where you'll learn how to navigate the boat. If you are comfortable on the "Cat", however, you can take it out on your own for a day or even two.

⊕ **Check it out:** SailSihanoukville.com

Take a Cooking Class

When in Cambodia, make Amok.

Sign up for the Tastes of Cambodia cooking class in Sihanoukville where you'll learn to make authentic Khmer dishes such as banana leaf salad, fresh spring rolls, fish amok, chicken red curry, and ginger dumplings. Vegetarians are also welcome! Just request a special menu in advance and Tastes of Cambodia will be happy to oblige.

⊕ **Check it out:** Facebook.com/TastesofCambodia

Yoga Retreat and Classes

After you fed your soul with long nights of partying and your body with crazy adventures on the water, consider slowing down for a few days at Vagabond Temple. This yoga center in Sihanoukville offers various retreats aimed towards various spiritual purposes. Some retreats focus on self-discovery and self-empowerment through ceremonies and life-coaching, while others work on detoxing your body and centering your energy with Reiki sessions and meditation.

PS. Take note that from May 27, 2017 – October 16, 2017, Vagabond Temple is closed for the rainy season.

⊕ **Check it out:** Vagabondtemple.com

CHAPTER 4: SIHANOUKVILLE

Crime & Safety in Sihanoukville

Little Thieves on Serendipity Beach
While you are getting all carefree with your cocktails on the beach, little beggar kids are getting to work. While you're distracted, they'll snatch your purse, wallet, or phone in a second. I would know…it happened to me.

Walking at Night
Stay on Serendipity Road near all the businesses and you'll be fine. Just steer clear of back roads and residential streets.

Responsible Drinking and Drug(ging?)
Whatever it is that you like to partake in, be it alcohol, ganja or something a bit stronger- do so with caution. Parties tend to get wild in Sihanoukville. The expats that live here are used to partying every night and make hardcore partying seem like a piece of cake. Don't try to keep up. Watch your pace. Keep your wits about you.

Police and Drugs
Right now, we have a friend sitting in the Sihanoukville jail/prison. She's doing some serious time after getting caught manufacturing drugs to resell. While I'm sure you aren't coming here to become a drug lord… just know that the police here are aware of foreigners' love for pills and weed. Don't carry it on your body or in your bag. Getting caught can be expensive…or worse.

PRO TIP: While it sounds like a stupid tip and an irresponsible tip- trust me when I say…if you're renting a motorbike and drive up on a police check point (usually near the Golden Lion round-about), don't stop. Don't make eye contact and just drive right by them or choose a different route.

CHAPTER 4: **SIHANOUKVILLE**

How to Get Around Sihanoukville

Walk
Each little area of Sihanoukville is walkable. By that I mean, whether you're staying in Otres 1 or on Serendipity Beach, there will be restaurants, bars, and tourism offices within walking distance from your hotel.

Tuk Tuk
This is a Tuk Tuk city! Getting around is made easy with $1 Tuk Tuk rides in Sihanoukville town and $5 Tuk Tuk rides between Serendipity and Otres.

TRAVEL NOTES:

....

....

....

....

....

CHAPTER 4: SIHANOUKVILLE

How to Get to Sihanoukville

FROM PHNOM PENH

By Plane
- **Point of Departure:** Phnom Penh Airport
- **When:** 12 flights per day
- **Duration:** 30 minutes
- **Budget:** Around $100

By Bus
- **Point of Departure:** Phnom Penh Bus Terminal
- **When:** All day every day
- → **For Giant Ibis:** Daily 8 am, 9:30 am and 12:30 pm
- **Duration:** 6-7 hours
- **Budget:** $4-10
- **Book:** www.12go.asia/en

By Private Taxi
- **Point of Departure:** Pick up at your hotel
- **When:** Whenever you want
- **Duration:** 4-5 hours
- **Budget:** Around $50 (depending on how you haggle)
- **Book:** Check out our section called 'Driver Directory' on page 225.

By Train
- **Point of Departure:** Phnom Penh Railway Station
- **When:** Friday at 3pm, Saturday at 7am, Sunday at 7 am, Monday at 4pm
- **Duration:** 6.5 hours (don't be surprised if the train is late)
- **Budget:** $7

FROM SIEM REAP

By Plane
- **Point of Departure:** Siem Reap Airport
- **When:** 12 flights per day
- **Duration:** 1 Hour
- **Budget:** Around $100

By Bus
- **Point of Departure:** Minivan or Tuk Tuk pick up from your hotel
- **When:** Daily at 7am
- **Duration:** 11-13 Hours
- **Budget:** $25

By Private Taxi
- **Point of Departure:** Pick up at your hotel
- **When:** Whenever you want
- **Duration:** 10 hours
- **Budget:** $120-150

FROM KAMPOT

By Minibus
- **Point of Departure:** Pick up from your hotel
- **When:** Daily 8 am, 11 am, 1:30 pm, 3:30 pm
- **Duration:** 2 hours
- **Budget:** $6

By Private Taxi
- **Point of Departure:** Pick up at your hotel
- **When:** Whenever you want
- **Duration:** 2 hours
- **Budget:** $30-40
- **Book:** Check out our section called 'Driver Directory' on page 225.

FROM THAILAND

By Bus
This trip can be completed in 3 back-to-back legs. It sounds really complicated, but the journey is well-traveled and runs smoothly with transport staff and Tuk Tuk drivers there to guide you.

1st Leg of the Trip: Bangkok to Trat
Point of Departure: Bangkok - Mo Chit Bus Terminal (Northern Bus Terminal) or Ekamai (Eastern Bus Terminal)
When: Daily 6am
Duration: 5-6 Hours
Budget: Around $8 USD

2nd Leg of the Trip: Trat to Hat Lek Border Crossing (Koh Kong)
Point of Departure: Trat Bus Terminal
When: Upon arrival
Duration: 1 Hour
Budget: $4-5 USD

3nd Leg of the Trip: Koh Kong to Sihanoukville
You'll take a $3 Tuk Tuk from Koh Kong border to the bus terminal – about 15km- then you'll hop on a bus. You're almost finished!

Point of Departure: Small Bus Terminal in Koh Kong
When: Daily at 1pm
Duration: 4 Hours
Budget: Around $7.50 USD

PRO TIP
Alternatively, you can hire a Taxi from the border or from the bus terminal to take you straight to Sihanoukville and skip all this bouncing around! Ask a few other travelers around you if they want to split the $50 fare for a much less stressful ride.

HEADS UP: At the border, there will be a desk with a big sign that says "quarantine" and some plainly clothed men sitting behind it. It's so obviously a scam that it's laughable. They'll tell you that you are required to get a "health check" which is them taking your temperature…and guess what! It will cost you $1. However, there is absolutely no law that states you need a health check. Seasoned expats have learned to ignore them and keep walking with a stern 'No' and a bit of confidence. Worse case…you don't feel comfortable saying no and you pay $1 to the corruption fund.

FROM THE AIRPORT IN SIHANOUKVILLE

When you land at the tiny airport in Sihanoukville, there will be Tuk Tuks and taxis who are ready to take you to your hotel. OR you can arrange a taxi ahead of time to pick you up.

Budget: Taxis are around $17 and Tuk Tuks are
Duration: The drive into town is about 20 minutes

From the Bus Station in Sihanoukville
The bus station is not within walking distance to town. You'll need to take a Tuk Tuk to your hotel or the Koh Rong pier.

Budget: The Tuk Tuk drivers will tell you $5 per person BUT if three or more people…don't pay more than $15 – this is the max rate you should pay.
Duration: 10 minutes

NOT SO FUN FACT
The average wage is less than $3 per day in Cambodia. The Khmers working at expat-owned bars and businesses, however, tend to be paid higher and work in more-enjoyable atmospheres.

PART TWO:

The Islands

PRO TIP:
Wear Bug Spray on the Beach.
Sand flies are all too common. They love to nibble your ankles when you walk- any time of day.

CHAPTER SIX

Koh Rong

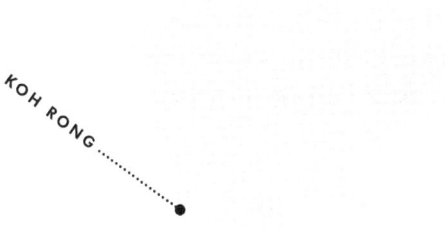

CHAPTER SEVEN

Koh Rong

A fishing village turned ultimate holiday destination, Koh Rong Island is the next big destination in South East Asia. Prepare to have your life changed.

With over 43 kilometers of white sand beaches, bathwater warm turquoise water, coconut trees lining the shore, and an eclectic mix of expats turned locals from all over the world- Koh Rong is the ultimate island vacation spot in Cambodia.

📷 @ THE.NATURALIST.VIEW

BEHIND THE SCENES:
A Cambodian Conglomerate has been granted a 99-year lease on the island with plans to turn Koh Rong into THE destination island in South East Asia for the richest of the rich. The island has gone from no cars or roads, to full-on plans of building an international airport. This cozy little secret will soon transform into a holiday-spot much like the bustling tourist islands of Thailand.

There is a reason why this island is so sought after… because it's magic. It feels like all the good energy in the universe meets right here. Ask anyone that has fallen in love with this island and they'll say the same thing. This is the "untouched island paradise" we all envision when we begin our SE Asian journey.

If you are lonely, you will feel like you've found family within a week. If you want to be alone, a beachside bungalow has a hammock with your name on it. If you are looking for an adventure, you can hike through the jungles for hours. And if you don't believe me, go see for yourself.

PRO TIPS FOR KOH RONG

HEADS UP: the following tips will make Koh Rong seem so icky. I'm aware. But this island is the opposite of icky. Koh Rong embodies quintessential island life with elements that usually wouldn't cross our mainland minds. The tips will prepare you to be an island baby from the moment you step off the boat. Here we go…

Bring Cash
There are no ATMs on Koh Rong and Debit Cards are not typically accepted by bars or guesthouses. Bring cash. If you run out of cash, Island Boys can work out a loan for you.

Take care of your Cuts
When you're barefoot 24/7, you're bound to get a scratch here and a bump there. And with the ocean mixed with sand and humidity- little cuts can

turn into infected situations real quick. It's important to keep your cuts clean. Almost every bar has a medical kit with cleaning solution and band aids that they'd be happy to let you use.

Don't Scratch your Bug Bites
Those will get infected, too.

You Might get Island Belly
It won't hurt. You'll just be pooping 3x a day. Embrace it. At least it keeps you from feeling bloated…right? Once you get back on the mainland, everything goes right back to normal, I promise.

Carry a Backpack
…instead of a rolley suitcase. It's pretty miserable dragging those things through the sand.

Take Short Showers
Even I have to remind myself sometimes that Koh Rong is an island with a limited clean water source.

AREAS TO EXPLORE ON KOH RONG

Koh Rong might be the size of Hong Kong, but it is relatively underdeveloped. No Tuk Tuk transportation here. Just white sand beaches and longtail boats.

Long Beach
On the other side of the mountain from Koh Toch Beach lies 7km of white sand paradise that is certainly worth the hike. Cool off in the turquoise water or grab a fresh fruit shake. As the day nears the end, groups of travelers gather on the shore to watch the gorgeous sunset. Once the sun is down, hike back or hop in a long tail boat waiting to take you back to the main beach.

Police Beach

Begin the morning on Police Beach when it's quiet. Plan to spend the day sunning in your bathing suit, playing in the water or joining in on a volleyball match. As the day carries on, the beach attracts a friendly crowd and now, the party has come to you.

To get here, no boats needed; just follow the well-trodden path past Green Ocean Guesthouse into the jungle and you'll come out on the other side at Police Beach.

Longset / 4k Beach

Walk to the far end of White Beach, through a flat jungle trail past some tall tree house bungalows and you'll reach Long Set Beach. Often called 4k Beach, this is the unspoiled paradise you've been looking for. Soft sand with turquoise water and overhanging coconut trees. Best of all, this beach is usually super quiet without the mainstream crowds.

FUN FACT: 4k Beach is so pristine that it was used as one of the campsites for a recent season of Survivor.

Sok San Village

The local residents of Sok San village have only recently decided to open their little beach community to backpackers. Located at the far end of Long Beach, away from the tourist trail on Koh Toch, you get the Khmer experience of drinking beers with locals, mingling with chickens, and entertaining curious kids. Best of all, unspoiled white sand beaches.

How to Get There: Take the Cambodia Island Speed Ferry from Sihanoukville to Sok San Long Beach (Open Return) for $27. Get off at that pier and walk 100 yards left."

CHAPTER 6: **KOH RONG**

Where to Stay in Koh Rong

Nest Beach Club

Brand new western-style air conditioned dorms are a god-send when all you want to do is escape the heat. Nest is one of the best kept secrets on Koh Rong. Here, you get the best of both worlds: modern facilities steps from the white sandy beach and local budget prices. This getaway is where many of the expats come to enjoy the 6-9pm Happy Hour and gather for live music nights and parties. Oh, and the beach is insane. In…sane.

★ **Style:** Dorms
Budget: $
Where: Walk to the end of White Beach, through the jungle path past Tree House Bungalows and you'll come out on Longset Beach, the home of Nest.

BOOK HERE

Coconut Beach Bungalows

Like staying at your best friend's place if that place was on a pristine beach in paradise. Your hosts, Pia and Robbie go out of their way to put a smile on your face and memories in your noggin. Choose between a futon tent or sea view bungalows. The beach is yours with hammocks and swings, crystal clear water, and photo ops for days. The beach is isolated but Robbie will help you book a quick $5 transfer from the main pier. The journey is worth it.

★ **Style:** Private Tent or Bungalow
Budget: $
Where: Coconut Beach

BOOK HERE

BeachWalk Koh Rong

Like a scene out of a movie, each private beach bungalow is nestled right in the sand just a few steps away from the water. Fall asleep to the sound of the waves crashing on the shore- but not before you splash with glowing plankton in the water at night. To get away from the boats and chickens, just take a short walk down the beach for pure isolation.

★ **Style:** Private Beach Bungalows
Budget: $$
Where: The end of Long Beach

BOOK HERE

Tree House Bungalows

A private beach in the jungle? How can you say no? As the name suggests, you'll find a collection of sturdy tree houses lining this tiny beach with balconies that offer unspoiled views of the ocean and unpolluted darkness at night for the most amazing star gazing. If the tree house is out of your budget, there are quiet bungalows tucked amidst the trees. On site is a bar and restaurant, as well as lounge chairs in the sand where you can get that nice vacay glow.

★ **Style:** Private Bungalows & Tree Houses
Budget: $
Where: At the end of White Beach through the jungle

BOOK HERE

Firefly Guesthouse

Off the beaten path you'll find this guest house on stilts over the water. Welcome to one of Koh Rong's original fishing villages where you can watch life go by from your balcony. Old boats, fascinating structures, and charming hospitality. If you want to travel like a local, bucket-showers and all, come here.

★ **Style:** Private Rooms and Dorms
Budget: $
Where: Prek Svay Village

BOOK HERE

CHAPTER 6: KOH RONG

Things to Do in Koh Rong

Sunbathe on White Sand Beaches
Right at the foot of Koh Rong's guesthouses, bars, and restaurants lies White Beach. It takes zero effort to crawl out of bed, throw on your suit and flop down under the sun with a towel and a good book. The sand is powdery soft and the sea is almost always bathwater warm. In between tanning sessions, you can run into the water to cool off. There are some shady palm trees for when you get too hot, vendors selling ice cold coconuts when you get thirsty, and volleyball nets when you get antsy.

PRO TIP: Don't swim too close to the piers as the water tends to be a bit dirty in that area.

Get your Open Water Diving Certificate
What girl doesn't love a bargain?! While the underwater visibility off Koh Rong isn't world-class, the price of Koh Rong's Open Water Diving Certificate certainly is. Your dives will be full of colorful fish, corals, urchins, sea horses and possibly even some manta rays. There aren't any wreck dives or cave sites but guess what? That's what allows this dive shop to fly under the radar in terms of price and small classroom size.

How Much: Starting at $260 USD
Where: The Main Pier on Koh Rong

Go Kayaking
You don't have to be a kayak pro to manage in these waters as they're pretty calm and you won't need to head too far out to sea in order to find adventure. Your best bet is to rent a kayak from one of the locals in Koh Toch village or over on Long Set beach at Sky and Sand bar. There is so

much exploring to be done around Koh Rong including "Small Island" which is visible from the main shore, mangroves over on Long Set beach, and nearby beaches like Police Beach.

💰 **How Much:** Just under $5 for a half day
📍 **Where:** All along White Beach

Swim with the Plankton

Do you remember the scene in the movie "The Beach" where Leo goes swimming in the bay as it lights up with glittery plankton? The same natural phenomenon occurs right here on Koh Rong! To get the best plankton experience, you need complete darkness. Walk as far from the lights of the beach as you can to find a blacked out strip of water or hire a boat to take you out at night for the ultimate glittery swim.

📷 @ KEV.WOLF

CHAPTER 6: KOH RONG

Nightlife in Koh Rong

Full Moon Party
Located in the idyllic beach cove of Police Beach, you can expect fully equipped sound systems with wild DJ's playing house, techno, and EDM, along with fire spinners and jugglers to keep you entranced. There's food to keep your energy going, drinks to keep your spirits high, and reasonably priced tickets for sale at the "door".

☉ **When:** Usually at the end of each month-

Police Beach Parties
Clear your busy island schedules Wednesday through Saturday (during high season) and get yourselves down to Police Beach where all night beach parties are in full swing til the sun comes up. DJ's, fire spinners, food, drinks- the whole scene is on point! Bring a flashlight and an extra beer for the walk over.

TRAVEL NOTES:

....

....

....

....

How to Get Around Koh Rong

Look down. You see those two cute little feet on the ground? That's your transportation. There are no beach roads here. It's all walkable.

If you want to get to another beach or make a day trip to Koh Rong Samloem, there is always a longtail boat for hire or a speed ferry that you can jump on!

Crime & Safety in Koh Rong

The biggest danger on the island is never leaving…because you'll love it that much. It happened to me. It can happen to you! Besides failing miserably in love with this place, you don't have toooooo much to worry about.

Violent crime isn't a big deal here. You'll have the occasional fight between drunk western guys but that's usually it.

Be aware of petty theft, keep your room locked when you leave, and don't hike the trails at night alone- just like you wouldn't do at home.

CHAPTER 6: **KOH RONG**

How to Get to Koh Rong

First, get your cute butt to Sihanoukville and book a ferry when you arrive. During high season, boats can fill up pretty quickly, so I recommend booking at least a day in advance so that you have more options in terms of what time you leave and arrive.

There are multiple speed boat companies that make getting to the island a breeze.

Book them at 12go.asia to check the times and book ☞

📍 **Where:** The main pier at the end of the bottom of the hill (you'll know what I'm talking about once you get to Sihanoukville).
🕒 **How Long:** 40-60 minutes (depending if they make a stop at Koh Rong Samloem).

PRO TIP
This chapter is about Koh Rong, the big island. Not Koh Rong Samloem (not yet, anyways). Sit tight. You're the last stop on the Speed Boat journey.

To book your return, simply go into the Dive Shop the day before (just to be safe) and let them know that you want to leave the next day. If you forget to do this, they'll let you hop on the boat as long as they have room.

A visit to Koh Rong is not a day trip – plan to spend at least 1 night on the island. You'll love it.

STORY TIME!

One morning, as I was sipping my coffee overlooking the serene beaches of Koh Toch Village, I saw a man sleeping face down in the sand. Quite out of place.

A few of us gathered him from the shore and noticed that he was still drunk at 8am.

We asked him, "Where are you staying, buddy?"

"Errr Sihanoukville"

"Okay, well you're on Koh Rong, my friend"

"No no…I'm in Sihanoukville"

"I can assure you…you are on Koh Rong"

Que the *"oh shit, my girlfriend is going to kill me"* on repeat. Turns out, he got so drunk that he got on the last ferry boat to the island…without his phone.

The end.

WANT MORE TRAVEL STORIES?

Join my Newsletter for more travel stories, travel tips and advice and more surprises to turn you into a pro traveler.

🌐 Visit SoloGirlsTravelGuide.com

CHAPTER SEVEN

Koh Rong Samloem

📷 @ALLPHOTOBANGKOK

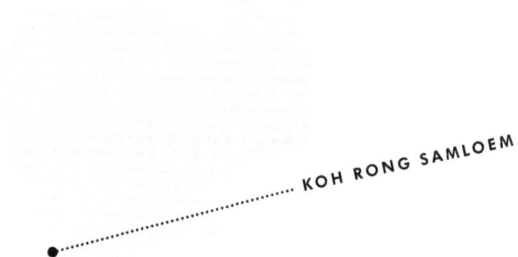

CHAPTER SEVEN

Koh Rong Samloem

Koh Rong's younger brother, Koh Rong Samloem is similar to what Koh Rong looked and felt like 5 years ago. With just a handful of guesthouses, a fraction of the tourist crowd, and only a couple boats docking on the island per day, come get a taste of that low-key island life.

Spend your days wandering the village while weaving around children playing and dogs napping in the sand, visit local restaurants for some traditional Khmer food, explore the jungle where you can see monkeys, Hornbills, and red squirrels, then pop into expat owned guest houses for a cold cider as the perfect end to a perfect day.

FUN FACT!

Have you seen many locals wearing scarves with gingham-like patterns? No, it's not that Cambodians are fans of gingham...these all-purpose-scarves are called Kramas and are a national symbol. They are usually made of cotton or silk and worn as headwraps, skirts, baby slips, sun shades...you name it.

AREAS TO EXPLORE ON KOH RONG SAMLOEM

M'Pai Bay

Right across from big Koh Rong is M'Pai Bay- which only started collecting expat-run guesthouses a few years ago. Island life for Khmers is still very much intact here. M'Pai Bay is a Cambodian community first and a tourist destination second with guest house owners very invested in creating a harmonious balance between the two. You can just as easily join a group of backpackers for a beer as you could join some Khmers drinking at a local minimart.

Saracen Bay

Get ready to make all of your friends jealous with an Instagram feed looking like you're vacationing with the Olsen Twins (or how I assume Billionaires vacation). Because holy moly, Saracen Bay will take your breath away. Powdery white sand beaches with bright turquoise water that remains shallow for a few meters out allowing you to bathe in the sun. This is one of my favorite places on Earth.

Sunset Beach

The name says it all! A chilled out slice of sand with only a couple guest houses, you don't have to battle crowds to get a piece of the pie. Consider staying on this corner of the island for solitude and silence.

MASSIVE PRO TIP...

There are no ATMs on Koh Rong and Debit Cards are not typically accepted. Bring cash. If you run out of cash, Bong's can work out a loan for you.

CHAPTER 7: KOH RONG SAMLOENG

Where to Stay in Koh Rong Samloem

✳ Saracen Bay offers more upscale accommodation- many with hot water showers, air-conditioning and solace.

✳ M'Pai Bay has that laidback backpacker vibe going on with cold showers, fan rooms and local watering holes where it's easy to chat with other travelers.

The One Resort

If you're chasing that idyllic postcard dream, look no further! The dream is alive at The One. High-end bungalows situated on pure white sand beaches that feel like walking on powder next to turquoise water that is as warm as it is clear, here's the ultimate get away. Jump from the ocean into the resort pool lined with cabanas with poolside food and drink service. I wish I could live here.

★ **Style:** Private Beach Bungalows

💰 **Budget:** $$$

📍 **Where:** Saracen Bay Beachfront

BOOK HERE

SunBoo Beach Bungalows

Want to stay on the most gorgeous beach in the country without blowing your whole travel fund? SunBoo Beach Bungalows has fan bungalows just steps from the beach at a price you can afford. This feels like staying at your friend's house…if your friend happened to live on one of the most beautiful islands in the world. Get ready for the best sunsets ever.

★ **Style:** Private Beach Bungalows
💲 **Budget:** $$
📍 **Where:** Sunset Beach

BOOK HERE

....

Longvek Guest House

Stay at Andrew's home. I met this vibrant Aussie expat one morning after I had suffered a crazy injury to my foot. He took a pen, a water bottle and a bottle of iodine and worked miracles to heal me - without even knowing my name. He's the kind of guy that gets excited to show you his favorite place for squid fishing, introduce all of his chickens by name, and share a home cooked dinner with everyone staying at his place. It's a social, family-feel that you won't forget.

★ **Style:** Privates
💲 **Budget:** $
📍 **Where:** M'Pai Bay
f Book on Facebook: Longvek Guesthouse

BOOK HERE

CHAPTER SEVEN: KOH RONG SAMLOEM

"If I'm an advocate for anything, it's to move. As far as you can, as much as you can. Across the ocean, or simply across the river. The extent to which you can walk in someone else's shoes or at least eat their food, it's a plus for everybody. Open your mind, get up off the couch, move."

— ANTHONY BOURDAIN

CHAPTER 7: KOH RONG SAMLOENG

Where to Eat in Koh Rong Samloem

Bongs

Bongs always have the best breakfast with breaky sausages, baked beans, bacon, baguettes…the works. Try the Fat Boy Breakfast to soak up all of the booze from the morning before. This is a place that will not pass judgment if you want to have a beer for breakfast. If that's too heavy for you, try the Espresso Martini or Bloody Mary.

Where: M'Pai Bay

Location: Directly at the end of the pier

Open: Breakfast to late

Erin's Kitchen

Home Cooked meals with a beachfront view. What more could you ask for? The cheerful Khmer staff at Erin's Kitchen are just getting used to the influx of tourists who seem to love what they're cooking up. Imagine making Amok Curry, Beef Lok Lak, and fruit pancakes your whole life, only to discover that these weird, tall gangly people from far away lands love it, too.

Where: M'Pai Bay

Location: The very left side of the beach – facing inland.

Open: Morning to night

Resorts Resorts Resorts

When you're staying on Saracen Bay, you've got plenty of high-end resorts to choose, all of which offer similar dishes at similar prices. You can find fresh fruit breakfasts, all of the curries for lunch, and plenty of seafood BBQ for dinner. Have a wander along the beach to pick out the atmosphere that pairs best with your appetite.

HEY! Do you know how many girls live their whole lives and never even leave their own country? Look at you go! You're special. Don't forget that.

TRAVEL NOTES:

....

....

....

....

....

CHAPTER 7: KOH RONG SAMLOENG

Things to Do on Koh Rong Samloem

Watch the Sunrise at M'Pai Bay Pier

It's tradition- for me at least. Right before dawn, I walk down to the pier and wake up with the sun. Bring your journal or a coffee and take the time to check back in with yourself while your feet dangle over the water, feeling like you're sitting at the edge of the Earth. When the sun is up, dive in for a soul-cleansing swim. Quiet, peaceful and relaxing.

Go Kayaking

Saracen Bay guest houses have kayaks for rent! It's typically $25 for 4 hours which gives you plenty of time to visit the mangroves, isolated beaches, fishing villages and nearby Rocky Island. Remember to wear sunscreen and bring a couple waters!

Take a Boat Trip around the Island

The best way to see all that the island has to offer is with a boat tour around the island. A Khmer boat captain will take you to fishing villages, isolated beaches, the lighthouse, and other must-see spots. You can snorkel or go fishing. You can even go swimming in the dark to splash around with the glowing plankton. Pop into Easy Tiger where they've got the best trips mapped out for you.

Take a Jungle Hike

Ask your guest house to point out some of the jungle paths that wind through the tall green trees and rolling hills. You can hike to the waterfall, go bird watching (cooler than it sounds) or venture to another beach. Just watch the clock- sun sets around 6

Get Day Drunk

I mean, why not?

Snuba

No, it's not a typo. Snorkel + Scuba = Snuba. Attached to a long air tube, this hybrid experience allows you to dive down below the surface to get up close with colorful fish and intricate corals. Visit the dive center for more info.

HAPPY OCEAN FACT!

The Koh Rong archipelago is home to Cambodia's first large-scale marine protection project. In any areas around Koh Rong and Koh Rong fishing is now regulated and the coral reef is being restored!

CHAPTER 7: **KOH RONG SAMLOENG**

Nightlife in Koh Rong Samloem

Full Moon Parties

..and Half Moon Parties and Black Moon Parties and 'Just Because' parties. Good Vibz Camp is a hippie haven located deep (ish) in the jungle between Saracen Bay and M'Pai Bay. It's a goddamn jungle party with live DJs, fire dancers, fluorescent paint, and travelers who have flocked from all corners of the country just to trade some amazing karma and have a good time! Don't miss this one. Check out their Facebook page to see dates and info!

BONUS: There's a free camping area and sleeping area so you don't have to worry about trekking back to your hotel after you've been partaking in party activities.

Bar Hop

There are 2 types of people on an isolated island with minimal wifi and no roads: those who day drink and those who should day drink. Start from one end of the beach and have a beer or cocktail at each guesthouse and local Khmer shop- collecting new friends and snacks along the way. Day bleeds into night and now you're night drinking like a responsible human. I knew you could do it.

Live Music Nights at Bongs

It's not every night or even every other night that there is live music at Bong's. But during High Season, the crew will throw a party with impressive musicians from around the globe. If you want to be that impressive musician and entertain the beach, shoot them a message. Live music guests get free drinks all night long.

CHAPTER 7: **KOH RONG SAMLOENG**

How to Get to Koh Rong Samloem

There are 2 ways to get to Koh Rong Samloem…

○ **Option 1: Start off in Sihanoukville**

And take a ferry (see the 'How to Get to Koh Rong' Section). Instead of buying a ticket to Koh Rong, buy yours to Koh Rong Samloem and specify which beach you want to go to: Saracen or M'Pai.

○ **Option 2: Start off on Koh Rong**

And take a boat to Samloem from there.

Here are your options for boating over…

→ Hire a private long tail boat from Koh Rong to Koh Rong Samloem for $25

→ Take a $7 Speed Ferry to M'Pai Bay: Everyday at 8am, 12pm, 1pm and 4pm

→ Take a $7 Speed Ferry to Saracen Bay: The times change all the time with the addition of new boats. But don't worry, there are multiple boats per day! Inquire on Koh Rong and you can schedule your ride over.

→ Jump on the $7 Long Tail Shuttle Boat leaving from Koh Toch every day at 12pm and 5pm – You can get tickets at the little stall in front of Rising Sun, called Bun Rong

And don't forget, you can make Koh Rong Samloem a quick day trip as well when you stay on big Koh Rong.

CHAPTER EIGHT

Koh Ta Kiev

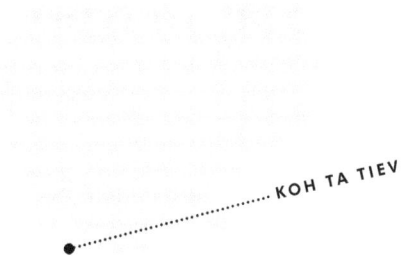

CHAPTER EIGHT

Koh Ta Tiev

If you are after a tropical island getaway to help you detach from the hustle and bustle of city life, Koh Ta Kiev is the answer. This island is quite remote and does not have internet connectivity. In other words, it's perfect! This paradise enables you to completely focus on the pristine scenery around you, instead of burying your nose in social media and techy gadgets.

With such a remote island, it's not surprising that there are only a handful of places to stay. And although the island isn't as developed as the other islands in Cambodia, Koh Ta Kiev still has some pretty cool options for accommodation. Let's take a look…

CHAPTER 8: KOH TA KIEV

Where to Stay in Koh Ta Kiev

Kactus

Kactus or "the Hidden Treehouse" is a beautiful paradise for the weary and adventurous. Located on the sunset side of Koh Ta Kiev, this beautiful paradise offers bungalows, dorms and even a simple hammock for your stay. The property is walking distance to a gorgeous private beach with dazzling gold sand and clear blue waters. Go kayaking or hiking during the day, and then enjoy cold Cambodian beer and yummy cuisine prepared by a talented French-Cambodian chef by night.

★ **Style:** Private Bungalows, Dorms, Hammocks
💰 **Budget:** $$
📍 **Where:** You can get here from Sihanoukville. Look for Kactus' boat station in front of Shop 41 on Ream beach. The boat leaves at 1 2:30pm for $7.50 per person, one way.

BOOK HERE

Crusoe Camping Island

Relax by the beach and camp out under the stars in total peace. This middle of nowhere spot is relatively unknown and unspoiled (until now, perhaps), so don't be surprised if you have the entire beach all to yourself. Rent a tent or cozy into bungalows with mesmerizing beach views. The site comes with an onsite restaurant which serves Asian and Western cuisine for affordable prices. You've got food, shelter, and stars. You're all set.

★ **Style:** Tents + Bungalows
💰 **Budget:** $
📍 **Where:** Look for "Rise" on Otres Beach and locate the ferry to the island
📍 **Where:** Long Beach

BOOK HERE

CHAPTER 8: KOH TA KIEV

Where to Eat in Koh Ta Kiev

With such isolated properties, it's no wonder that restaurants don't exist. Rather, each guesthouse and hostel have their own restaurants with fresh ingredients and yummy snacks. How convenient!

If you need cheese, chocolate, or a bag of chips, stock up before you come to the island!

Things to Do in Koh Ta Kiev

Do Nothing

That's the whole appeal of Koh Ta Kiev. The ability to do absolutely nothing here. Often on vacation, we still feel pressure and urgency to do and see everything on our checklist. But not here. Unplug and unwind. Remember what it feels like to wake up with no plans or responsibilities. Get in touch with yourself. Connect back with nature. And occasionally, enjoy the company of other travelers who are looking for that same feeling.

Plan Ahead

Rent or buy a book from Idle Hour Bookshop before you head on out to Koh Ta Kiev. With a vast collection of books available in various languages, there's something here for everyone. You can rent a book for your island stay or buy one to swap at a guest house's book library in the future. In addition to books, Idle Hour Bookshop also sells games, stationery and 2nd-hand clothes. You'll find this quaint little library in Otres 1, just in front of The Greenhouse Effect.

Visit Bamboo Island (Koh Ruessei)

Island hopping is a must while staying in a tropical country! While staying on Koh Ta Kiev, hop over to the neighboring island of Koh Ruessei. Known for its fine pink sand beaches and virgin forests- it's unlike any island you've ever seen. Stroll the beach collecting shells, sun bathing and enjoying being on one of the last pristine islands in the world. There is a super luxury resort here that starts at around $2k per night. It's fun to try and catch a peek of how these people vacay.

Explore Ream National Park

Opened in 1993, this national park hosts some of the country's most endangered and threatened natural resources: from animals to flora. For those after a challenge, the national park has various trekking routes within its 6,000-hectare territory. Bird watching is spectacular (even if you think that you're not into that kind of thing) and the jungle feels like something out of a CGI Disney movie. Unreal.

Check out Otres Beach

Otres Beach is a popular jumping off point to reach Koh Ta Kiev- so why not take a day or two to relax here before you dive into isolation? With tons of restaurants, lively bars, and beaches that are perfect for a day of laying out in the sun, here is a nice place to transition your brain from city mode to remote island mode.

Take a Day Trip to Koh Rong Samloem

Koh Rong Samloem is actually one of the newest tourist destinations in the Sihanoukville province. This island is similar to Koh Ta Kiev in terms of its unspoiled environment, but is starting to gather a pretty wonderful expat community. With that expat community comes great food, fun mountain biking tours, boat trips, and local Khmers who are happy to welcome western guests.

CHAPTER 8: KOH TA KIEV

How to Get to Koh Ta Kiev

FROM SIHANOUKVILLE
– THAT'S THE ONLY WAY!

By Boat

📍 **Point of Departure:** Most resorts Otres Beach (ask your hotel, they'll know where)

🕐 **When:** Daily at 10-11:30am

🕐 **Duration:** 1 Hour

💰 **Budget:** $10-$13 Round-trip

PRO TIP

During high season, join an island hopping tour that visits Koh Ta Kiev. It is possible to ask the tour boat to drop you off on Koh Ta Kiev for 1 or 2 nights. You'll hop back on their boat when they visit next.

♥ Coming to Cambodia and have questions, want some tips or just want to chat about life in South East Asia?

Reach out to me on Instagram @SoloGirlsTravelGuide

♥ Want to live in Cambodia?

Visit my blog to learn how to become a teacher here.

www.TheSoloGirlsTravelGuide.com

BONUS!

Volunteering in Cambodia

📷 MOVETOCAMBODIA

As I've mentioned once before, you must take extreme caution when deciding to volunteer in Cambodia – particularly with children. "Volun-tourism" is a massive industry that is both misleading to the well-intentioned travelers who want to do a good deed and exploitive to impoverished families here in Cambodia who are all too often taken advantage of.

An easy key to decipher whether an organization is moral is this: if any organization allows you to spend 1 day, 1 week, 2 weeks, 3 weeks, a month with their school children/orphanage/rescued sex workers/street children…they are exploiting those people for your money, donation, or "room and board fee".

Before volunteering with children or formerly abused people in Cambodia, ask yourself these questions….

✳ How is my involvement contributing to this organization?

✳ Has this organization just let you (a stranger) walk straight into an environment with vulnerable at risk children and adults?

✳ If you pay for your experience – how much of that cash actually benefits the children or people involved?

Fact: Hundreds of organizations around Cambodia exist solely to profit from volun-tourism. The children and women rarely see or feel a penny.

To truly leave a positive mark on Cambodia, here is a list of fabulous organizations around the country that offer beautiful opportunities for outsiders to immerse themselves in the local culture, make a sustainable difference, and support a well-deserving cause.

Marine Conservation Center in Kep

Nature lovers can get in on sustainable conservation projects that directly impact sustainable environmental practices here in the south of Cambodia. From marine research on seahorse populations to actually joining patrol teams that survey the waters watching for illegal fishing and poaching- this organization is ready for you to come help. MCC also offers academic internships for students of conservation, marine science and related areas!

🌐 **Contact:** MarineConservationCambodia.org

Phare Circus in Siem Reap

Helping young Khmer artists realize their dreams of performing, the fabulous Phare Circus needs techy and social media savvy volunteers! This is a great role for Digital Nomads who can commit to long term projects for 3 - 6 months. In return, Phare provides a living stipend of 100 USD per month and covers your visa extension fee during the whole period of contract. Plus…admission to the Phare circus family.

🌐 **Contact:** PhareCircus.org

Bartend Anywhere!

5 years ago, I landed on the shores of Koh Rong without any travel (or bartending) experience under my belt. I planned to stay on the island for 2 days…I ended up staying a month. That's because within an hour of arriving on Koh Rong, I somehow landed a bartending job at Island Boys (I was one of the first Island Girls ever, no big deal). With that bartending job came a built in family of travelers that inspired me and empowered me to live this life of traveling the world. My life was literally never the same.

That first month eventually turned into 5 years of on and off Cambodia living, hence why I am writing this book. But that's a story for another time….

There's always a bar hiring in Siem Reap, Phnom Penh, Kampot, Sihanoukville, Koh Rong and beyond that typically require a 3 week+ commitment. You get a free room, food, and drinks. Do it.

ITINERARIES FOR
Cambodia

Cambodia is the kind of destination that is best without a fixed schedule. I'm about to fly to Cambodia next week and all I have booked is my first hotel in Kampot and my driver from the Phnom Penh airport to Kampot.

I will spend two months hopping around on a bucket list, rather than an itinerary. I'll book my hotels a day or two in advance when I'm sure that is the direction I'm headed.

BUT if you're on a fixed schedule, you might want a more solid plan, right?

It is possible to hop around the entire country in a couple weeks if you're open to flying.

But if you plan to bus it - don't try to be a hero and see it all! You can do it, but it will be miserable. Instead, consider squeezing as much as you can get out of a couple destinations, rather than skimming the surface of every location.

No matter your situation, I've got you covered.

Want me to plan your trip for you?
I make Bucket List Vacations come true.
Visit the Trip Planning section on TheSoloGirlsTravelGuide.com

PLAN YOUR TRIP...

Itineraries for Cambodia

Here's how to map out your schedule on a time-budget:

1 WEEK OPTIONS
1 Week — Siem Reap and Phnom Penh
1 Week — Kampot and Koh Rong
1 Week — Koh Rong and Koh Rong Samloem

2 WEEKS
Siem Reap — 3 Days
Phnom Penh — 2 Days
Sihanoukville — 2 Days
Koh Ron — 4 Days
Koh Rong Samloem — 3 Days

3 WEEKS - THE WHOLE DAMN COUNTRY
→ 3 Days in Siem Reap
→ 2 Days in Phnom Penh
→ Take the 7am train to Kampot
→ 3 Days in Kampot
→ Take a Bus or Taxi to Sihanoukville - Get straight on the ferry to Koh Rong
→ Spend 4 days on Koh Rong (change hotels once)

→ Take a longtail boat over to Koh Rong Samloem
→ Spend 4 days on Koh Rong Samloem (change hotels once)
→ Head back to Sihanoukville
→ 1 night in Sihanoukville, Otres Beach
→ Boat to Koh Ta Kiev
→ 2 nights Koh Ta Kiev
→ Back to Sihanoukville to leave Cambodia by bus or Plane

☞ You've got a couple wiggle days here. Don't book your hotels or transportation too far in advance so that if you want to stay somewhere a day longer, you can.

WANT A CUSTOMIZED ITINERARY?

I create dream vacations based on your Travel Bucket List!

Find out more at TheSoloGirl'sTravelGuide.com/Trip-Plans or message me directly at hello@thesologirlstravelguide.com

WHERE NEXT...

How to Get to Other Countries

TO THAILAND

Bangkok is going to be your landing point in Thailand! Spend a few fun days there and then jet off towards elephants in the jungle up north or monkeys on the beach down south.

Check out my Cambodia guides on Amazon to plan the best adventure ever filled with pro tips and money saving secrets.

PRO TIP: Always choose Giant Ibis for the safest and most comfortable long distance journeys.

By Minivan from Phnom Penh
- *Point of Departure:* It depends on the companies! Ask your booking agent.
- *When:* Daily at 5am
- *Duration:* 11.5 hours
- *Budget:* $26

By Bus from Phnom Penh
- *Point of Departure:* Giant Ibis Bus Terminal
- *When:* Daily at 8 pm, 9 pm, 9:30 pm
- *Duration:* 11 hours
- *Budget:* $23

By Bus from Sihanoukville
- *Point of Departure:* Sihanoukville Bus Station

- **When:** Daily at 8:30pm
- **Duration:** 10 hours
- **Budget:** $25

By Bus from Siem Reap
- **Point of Departure:** Giant Ibis Bus Terminal
- **When:** Daily at 7:45am
- **Duration:** 8.5 hours
- **Budget:** $32

By Plane from any International Airport in Cambodia
- **When:** Multiple flights per day
- **Duration:** About 1 hour
- **Budget:** Anywhere from $50-100

TO LAOS
By Bus from Phnom Penh

There are multiple minivans and buses that travel to Ho Chi Minh everyday. For safety and comfort, you know which company I'm recommending…Giant Ibis (duh).

- **Point of Departure:** Giant Ibis Bus Terminal
- **When:** Daily at 8 am and 12:30 pm
- **Duration:** 6.5-7 hours
- **Budget:** $18

By Plane
The routes you can take are:
→ Siem Reap > Pakse (Stopover)
→ Siem Reap > Luang Prabang (Direct)
→ Phnom Penh > Vientiane (Direct)

- **When:** Multiple flights per day
- **Duration:** All flights are under 2 hours
- **Budget:** Anywhere from $70-400

TO VIETNAM

PRO TIP: Be sure to apply for a Vietnamese Visa a few days in advance! You can do this at any tourist agency in Cambo or online.

By ground, you will travel to Ho Chi Minh, formerly known as Saigon, in the south of Vietnam. By air, you can fly to any city with an international airport.

By Bus from Phnom Penh

There are multiple minivans and buses that travel to Ho Chi Minh everyday. For safety and comfort, you know which company I'm recommending…Giant Ibis (duh).

- **Point of Departure:** Giant Ibis Bus Terminal
- **When:** Daily at 8 am and 12:30 pm
- **Duration:** 6.5-7 hours
- **Budget:** $18

NOTE: You can take buses from Sihanoukville, Kampot, and Siem Reap – but they will all pass through Phnom Penh.

By Plane

- **When:** Multiple flights per day
- **Duration:** 45 minutes - 1 hour
- **Budget:** Anywhere from $60-100

THINGS TO KNOW...

Cambodian Festivals & Holidays

A little festival incentive to help you plan your big trip!

JANUARY

December 31st — January 1st: *Western New Year*

Cities and islands that have been dusted with international influence put on big New Years parties and celebrations just like back home. On a bigger scale, bars and clubs will go all out with DJs, drink specials, and festive decor. On a smaller scale, you might find Khmer kids in the streets with illegal fireworks! Bring something sparkly and plan to stay up until midnight.

Best Place to Celebrate...
* Koh Rong Island – All of it!
* Phnom Penh Western Hotels like Sofitel or Sokha
* Phnom Penh Clubs like Vito or Heart of Darkness

January 7th: Victory over Genocide Day

The Khmer Rouge fell on January 7th, 1979. While this is a celebratory day for most Khmer people, it can be a contentious day for Khmers who found themselves fighting alongside the regime. Regardless, it's a monumental day for the country's history- particularly in Phnom Penh where you can attend a gathering and parade where military and civilians gather to listen to speeches and presentations. You might not understand every word, but you'll certainly feel the sentiments and emotion.

Best Place to Commemorate...
* Koh Pich in Phnom Penh

End of January (depending on the moon): *Meak Bochea*

On this full-moon day, Buddhists repent from their mistakes and sins by visiting temples for special ceremonies and gathering for massive parades in the streets. To honor Buddha and his teachings, you'll witness traditions and rituals with chanting, incense and candles on a fascinating large scale.

Best Spot to Celebrate...
* Tuol Sleng Genocide Museum (Phnom Penh) to witness repenting
* Preah Reach Trop Mount in Ponhea Leu District for a parade
* Both big and small Buddhist Temples around Cambodia

FEBRUARY

January 22nd, 2023: *Chinese New Year*

While there are plenty of Chinese-Khmer citizens in Cambodia, there isn't a central China Town for celebrations. Rather, those celebrating Chinese New Year celebrate in a small family setting.

PRO TIP: If you can, avoid visiting during Chinese New Year. Cambodia is the new hot spot destination for Chinese Tour Groups. With direct flights from China, you can expect the beaches to be crowded, hotels to be overbooked, ferry boats to fill up in advance, and airports to be an absolute shit show.

MARCH

March 8th: *International Women's Day*

Cambodian women are a force to be reckoned with! Most countries that have been struck by unimaginable tragedy remain broken. But not Cambodia. Thanks largely to the women of this country who got to work quickly, repairing business, healing families, and inspiring cultural growth and change. Women's day celebrates women of all ages! It's a beautiful day to be in Cambodia.

Most Popular Celebration Spots...

✷ Koh Rong Island – The local organization 'Friends of Koh Rong' throws an annual celebration of women and girls on the island. Gather in the village to witness and join in on the empowerment of local ladies.

APRIL
April 14th - 17th: *Khmer New Year (Chol Chnam Thmey)*

Get ready for 3 days of beer, whiskey, and baby powder. Yes, baby powder. Khmers cover each other in this stuff and carry on drinking while looking like ghosts. Night time feasts are common and music lasts well into mid-morning until the beer lulls everyone to sleep.

→ **Day 1:** Maha Sangkran- a day to pay homage to Buddha by visiting temples

→ **Day 2:** Vireak Vanabat- the day of charity and donations

→ **Day 3:** Vearak Loeng Sak- A day to wash away sins by washing Buddhist statues and pouring clean water on the elderly

Most Popular Celebration Spots...

✷ Wat Phnom in Phnom Penh for traditional ceremonies

✷ Visit small villages or small corner stores where locals will be drinking (and would love for you to join)

✷ My Personal Recommendation: Koh Rong Samloem Village. From the pier, go left in the sand and keep walking until you go over a tiny bridge. You'll enter the village where you can join in on a day of drinking and dancing with the locals!

OCTOBER
October 13th: *Pchum Ben (Ancestor's Day)*

It is believed that on this day, spirits and ancestors come down from the heavens to visit family members and friends. The living visit pagodas, offering food, incense and money to help ease spirits' burdens and connect with their loved ones who have passed. Business and government offices shut down while temples fill up.

Most Popular Celebration Spots...

✷ Angkor Wat

✷ Temples and pagodas of all sizes

October 29th: *Coronation Day*

Not exactly like Elsa's party in Frozen, but still well worth a trip to the palace- Coronation Day marks the anniversary of when King Norodom Sihamoni took the throne. The Royal Palace is lit up and decorated with extra special touches!

Most Popular Celebration Spot...

✷ Phnom Penh's Royal Palace

NOVEMBER

November 9th - *Independence Day*

Ceremonies in the morning and fireworks in the evening- Cambodia's Independence Day is done right. Commemorating Cambodia's independence from France and paying tribute to King Sihanok who is credited for reaching independence, this is a fantastic opportunity to soak up some history.

Most Popular Celebration Spots...

✷ Phnom Penh's Independence Monument in the morning

✷ Phnom Penh's Riverfront in the evening

November 26-28th 2023 - *Bon Om Touk Water Festival*

Dragon Boat Races! To celebrate the end of the rainy season and to say 'thank you' to the rivers that give life to this country- millions of Khmers gather in the capitol! For 3 days, there are boat races, concerts, parades and a special rice treat called Ak Ambok that is specially made.

Most Popular Celebration Spot...

✷ Tonle Sap River that runs in front of the Royal Palace

MINI Directory
FOR CAMBODIA

IMPORTANT STUFF

Tourist Police – English Speaking
PHNOM PENH
Phone: 012 942 484
Address: St. 598, 12107, Phnom Penh

SIEM REAP
Phone: 012 402 424
Address: Mondul 3 Village, Sangkat Slor Kram

Royal Phnom Penh Hospital – *For Serious Injury*

Western standards- more expensive than other Cambodian hospitals but cheaper than American hospitals!
Phone: 023 991 000
Address: 888 Russian Confederation Blvd, Teuk Thla, Phnom Penh

Travellers Medical Clinic – *$40 per Visit*
Phone: 023 306 802
Address: 88 Street 108 (Wat Phnom Quarter), Phnom Penh

EMBASSIES

American Embassy
Emergency Line: 023 728 000
Address: 1 Christopher Howes (96), Phnom Penh, Cambodia

British Embassy
Emergency Line: 023 213 470
Address: National Assembly Street, Phnom Penh, Cambodia

Canadian Embassy
Emergency Line: 023 213 470
Address: Street 254 (Senei Vinnavat Oum), House #9

Australian Embassy
Emergency Line: 023 213 470
Address: National Assembly Street, Phnom Penh, Cambodia

CAMBODIA DRIVER DIRECTORY

PHNOM PENH

Phnom Penh Cab Driver
🚌 *Transportation:* Car
f *Facebook:* phnompenhcabdriver
👥 *Capacity:* 1-4 people

Mr. Leang
🚌 *Transportation:* Car
📱 *Whatsapp:* +855 69 678 377
👥 *Capacity:* 1-4 people

....

SIEM REAP

Mr. Lem
🚌 *Transportation:* Tuk Tuk
📍 *Area:* Siem Reap
📱 *WhatsApp:* +855885473246
f *Facebook:* Lem Live
👥 *Capacity:* 1-4 people

Mr. Samith
Transportation: Tuk Tuk
📍 *Area:* Siem Reap
📱 *Phone Number:* +85569221250
👥 *Capacity:* 1-4 people

....

KAMPOT

Pharith Yin
🚌 *Transportation:* Car
f *Facebook:* facebook.com/pharithyin

MORE...

Mr. La
🚌 *Transportation:* Lexus RS
📍 *Area & Route:* Sihanoukville to Phnom Penh (or within these cities)
📱 *Phone Number:* +885464432 / +98 63 58 71
👥 *Capacity:* 4 People

Mr. Dara
🚌 *Transportation:* Lexus RS
📍 *Area & Route:* Kampot to Phnom Penh (or within these cities)
📱 *Phone Number:* 0777 77 20 21 / 017 89 19 81
👥 *Capacity:* 4 People

....

When these drivers are booked up, they will often send one of their Taxi driver friends in their place. It's a country full of wonderful hustlers and hard workers!

For more drivers or to schedule a ride share with other travelers, check out the Facebook group called '**Taxi Share Cambodia**'.

GYNECOLOGY SERVICES & FEMALE STUFF

Women's Center (OB/GYN) | Khema Clinic and Maternity

All of the services including birth control, ultrasounds, STD testing, Pap smears, etc.

Open: Daily 24/7
Phone: 023 880 949
Address: 18 Street 528, Toul Kork, Phnom Penh

Birth Control Pills

You can buy birth control pills over the counter in Cambodia. Look for tested brands called FMP, OK, Anna or Microgynon ED.

⚲ Where: All pharmacies

Other Birth Control Methods

The patch, IUDS, Shots and more can be found at many English-speaking clinics around the country- and usually for a cheaper price than back home.

⚲ Where: Reproductive Health Association of Cambodia (RHAC), Khema Clinic and Maternity, & Marie Stopes International are recommended by female expats.

Morning After Pill

⚲ Where: Most pharmacies carry these pills under "Pregnon" (I know, right?) or "Anlitin" for around $5

Unwanted Pregnancy

⚲ Where: Marie Stopes International

Legal up to 12 weeks but not widely available.

Locations in Phnom Penh, Siem Reap and Battambang

✉ Contact: hotline@mariestopes.org.kh

Medical Abortion Pill – Metabon

⚲ Where: Pharmacies carry this pill which is effective for up to 9 weeks after pregnancy. I recommend calling or consulting a clinic before you take the pill.

For more information, check out gynopedia.org/Cambodia

THE TRUE STORY OF HOW THE
Solo Girl's Travel Guide
WAS BORN

I was robbed in Sihanoukville.

Sure, the robber was a child and yes, I might have drunkenly put my purse down in the sand while flirting with an irresistible Swedish boy…but that doesn't change the fact that I found myself without cash, a debit card and hotel key at 1am in a foreign country.

My mini robbery, however, doesn't even begin to compare to my other travel misadventures. I've also been scammed to tears by taxi drivers, idiotically taken ecstasy in a country with the death penalty for drugs and missed my flight because how was I supposed to know that there are two international airports in Bangkok?

It's not that I'm a total idiot.
It's just that…people aren't born savvy travelers.

I'm not talking about hedonistic vacationers who spend their weekend at a resort sipping Mai Tais. I'm talking about train-taking, market-shopping, street food-eating travelers!

Traveling is not second (or third or fourth) nature; it's a skill that only comes with sweaty on-the-ground experience…especially for women!

In the beginning of my travels (aka the first 5 years), I made oodles of travel mistakes. And thank god I did. These mistakes eventually turned me into the resourceful, respected and established travel guru that I am today.

Year-after-year and country-after-country, I started learning things like...

✓ Always check your hostel mattress for bed bugs.

✓ Local alcohol is usually toxic and will give you a hangover that lasts for days.

✓ The world isn't "touristy" once you stop traveling like a tourist.

✓ And most importantly, the best noodle shops are always hidden in back alleys.

After nearly 11 years of traveling solo around the world (4 continents and 26 countries, but who's counting?) – I travel like a gosh darn pro. I save money, sleep better, haggle harder, fly fancier, and speak foreign languages that help me almost almost blend in with the locals despite my blonde hair.

Yeah yeah yeah. I guess it's cool being a travel icon. But shoot...

Do you know how much money, how many panic attacks, and how many life-threatening risks I could have saved and/or avoided if only someone had freakin' queued me into all of this precious information along the way? A lot. A lotta' lot.

So, why didn't I just pick up a travel guide and start educating myself like an adult? I had options...right? I could've bought a copy of Lonely Planet...but how the hell am I supposed to smuggle a 5-pound brick in my carry-on bag? Or DK Eyewitness, perhaps? Hell no. I don't have 8 hours to sift through an encyclopedia and decode details relevant to my solo adventure.

There was no travel guide that would have spared my tears or showed me how to travel safer and smarter.

The book I needed didn't exist. So, I freakin' wrote it myself.

What travel guide do you need me to write next?
Tell me on Instagram ♥ @SoloGirlsTravelGuide

Have any feedback? Love the book? Have a cool story?
Want to see something in the book that isn't there?
There's always room for love and improvement.
Reach out to me and let me know!

Send me your best photo from your trip in Cambodia.
I feature the best ones on my social media every week!

This one is from @rosieposie055 in Thailand.
Extra points if your travel guide is in the photo!

THE 11 TRAVEL COMMANDMENTS
OF Solo Girl's Travel Guide

01 Be an Explorer, Not a Tourist.

Some people travel just for the photo. While others travel to find the unfamiliar, connect with strangers, expand their minds, and try new things for the sake of trying new things. Which kind of traveler are you?

02 Leave Room for Happenstance

Don't overstuff your itinerary. Slow down, be where you are and leave room for serendipity! Literally, schedule serendipity time so the universe can take the lead.

03 Vote with your Dollar

When possible, choose to support local businesses that operate ethically - aka businesses that respect the environment, benefit their local communities, don't take advantage of animals and just treat their staff really really well.

04 Look for the Gift

Love your mistakes! With every bump in the road comes a gift. Miss a bus? Look for the gift. Lose your room key? Look for the gift. Get dumped on your honeymoon? Look for the gift! There will always be a gift.

05 Stay Curious

Ask questions! Ask questions when you like something and ask questions when you don't understand something. Out loud or in your head. And whenever you feel judgment arise, replace it with a question instead.

06 More Stories, Less Photos

Take a couple photos and then put your phone away. While everyone else is taking shitty sunset photos that never look as good on camera…you are really there, experiencing every shade of color in real time. Take note in your head of the story you will bring home - of the people you see, the food you smell, the monkeys in the trees! Look up, not down.

07 Count Experiences, Not Passport Stamps

You can never "do" Mexico. You can go to Mexico 50 times and still each experience will be different than the last. Travel to live, not to brag.

08 Mind your Impact

Leave every place better than you found it. Take a piece of trash from the beach and be kind to people you meet. Bring your own water bottle, canvas bag, and reusable straw to avoid single-use plastics.

09 Avoid Voluntourism

People are not zoo animals. Playing with children at orphanages, temporarily teaching English in villages or volunteering at women's shelters hurt more than they help. Want to volunteer with a positive impact? Check out my blog at TheSoloGirlsTravelGuide.com/travel-blog

10 Carry your Positivity

Ever had a crappy day and then a stranger smiles at you and flips your entire mood? Travel can be hard, but your positivity will be your secret weapon. Happy vibes are contagious. Even when we don't speak the local language, a smile or a random act of kindness tips the universal scale in the right direction for you and the people you meet along your journey.

11 Trust your Gut

Listen to that little voice inside you. When something doesn't feel right, back away. When something feels good, lean. Your intuition will lead you to beautiful places, unforgettable moments, and new lifelong friends.

BONUS: Drink where the Locals Drink, Eat Where the Locals Eat

Even if it's under a tarp outside a mini mart. This is how you discover the best food and make the most meaningful connections.

It feeeeeeeels good to travel good.

A CONFESSION:

I bend the rules. Sometimes I stay in an all-inclusive resort instead of a locally owned guesthouse. Sometimes I go to McDonalds because I want a taste of home. And sometimes, especially when I'm tired or hungry, I'm not all sunshine and rainbows to be around.

But my moral travel compass does not bend for things that matter to me. I'll never leave a piece of trash on the beach. I'll never support elephant riding. I'd rather stay home than go on a Carnival Cruise even if it was free. Decide what matters to you now, let that guide you as you travel but let yourself be human.

Comfort yourself when you need comforting and eat the forbidden fruit sparingly. When you do make mistakes, brush yourself off and do better next time. No one's path is perfect but I'm proud of you for making your path better.

THIS TRIP.
THIS IS WHEN YOU DISCOVER EXACTLY WHO YOU ARE.
TRUST YOURSELF.

JOIN THE

SOLO GIRL'S
REVIEW CLUB

TEST AND REVIEW OUR BOOKS AND MERCH

BE THE FIRST TO GET NEW BOOKS, TOTE BAGS AND MORE TRAVEL GOODIES

SECRET ACCESS STARTS HERE

DID YOU LEAVE A REVIEW?

As a self-published author – doing this whole publishing thing by myself – reviews are what keeps The Solo Girl's Travel Guide growing.

If you found my guidebook to be helpful,
please leave me a review on Amazon.com

Your review helps other girls find this book
and experience a truly life-changing trip.

Ps. I read every single review.

Leave me a review here — it will just take a sec!

ACKNOWLEDGMENTS

♥ To Emilia

You bring my visions to life! Thank you for designing this book. I can't wait to take it and travel to Cambodia with you.

♥ To The Solo Girl's Review Club

The girls who test everything I make and create, you are my inspiration! Your ideas and positive encouragement mean the world to me. Thank you for helping me create only the best resources for girls around the world.

♥ To Every Girl that Has Messaged Me

Or left me a review telling me how these books have impacted you – thank you for reminding me that travel changes people, that these books change people.

I LOVE YOU ALL!
WOMEN SUPPORTING WOMEN IS HOW MAGIC HAPPENS.

PASS IT ON!

This guide book is meant to change lives.
Don't let it sit on a shelf forever and ever.

Before you give this book to a friend
who needs a travel push
or before you leave it in the hostel
for the next travel girl to find…

On the back cover…

✧ write your name,
✧ your Instagram,
✧ and the dates you traveled.

This is your legacy, too.

xoxo, Alexa

WHERE NEXT?

BALI   **THAILAND**   **MEXICO CITY**

SOUTH KOREA   **JAPAN**   **VIETNAM**

And More...
Get The Whole Collection.

Lightning Source UK Ltd.
Milton Keynes UK
UKHW021301300123
416178UK00021B/806